PRAISE FOR STEVE SILVERMAN AND
WHO'S BETTER,
WHO'S BEST IN FOOTBALL?, 2009 Edition

"Steve Silverman has forgotten more about pro football than most of us will ever know. But that doesn't mean you won't disagree with his *Who's Better, Who's Best* list. Dick Butkus ahead of Lawrence Taylor? No way! You may not always see eye-to-eye with Steve, but you'll definitely learn something. So crack open this smart and provocative book and let the fun begin."

> —Allen St. John, *New York Times* best-selling author of
> *The Billion Dollar Game*

"You may not agree with all of Silverman's choices, but you will have to agree on how well he makes the case for his choices. When the official list comes out for Who's Better, Who's Best of all football books, Silverman's book will have to be a the top of the list."

> —Allen Barra, columnist, *The Wall Street Journal*

"No Steelers in the top 15? C'mon Steve. But don't hold it against this book. If you enjoy reading about football, and arguing about your favorite players, this is the place to be."

> —Ed Bouchette, columnist, *Pittsburgh Post-Gazette*

"Steve Silverman has smashed open a hornet's nest of controversy over his selections in *Who's Better, Who's Best in Football?* He makes excellent cases for his top 60 players even when one disagrees violently with his choices. The read is provocative as well as thought provoking."

> —Jeff Davis, author of *Papa Bear* and *Rozelle*

"Picking the top 60 players in NFL history seems an impossible task. Steve Silverman takes it a step further by listing them in order, an infuriatingly subjective process sure to divide football fans of any one team let alone the NFL. Who is the best Chicago Bears player ever? Dick Butkus, Mike Ditka, Gale Sayers, and Walter Payton make the list, but in what order and with how many other legends between them? Silverman's sharply written book will cause more arguments than it solves."

—Mike Mulligan, WSCR-AM morning host

"I love books like this, books that get the arguments going. Steve Silverman has a good one here, except I must take exception with Joe Montana over Jim Brown. Plain and simple, Brown was the greatest football player of all-time and I'm not even sure Montana's the best quarterback. But the book is great."

—Mike Shalin, co-author of *Out by a Step: The 100 Best Players Not in the Baseball Hall of Fame*

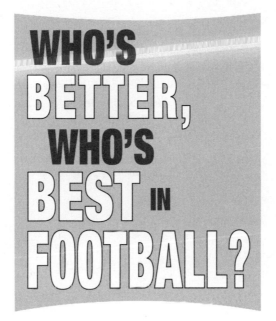

Also by Steve Silverman

The Good, The Bad and The Ugly: Minnesota Vikings
The Good, The Bad and The Ugly: Philadelphia Eagles
Then Steve Said to Jerry
The Story of the Indiana Pacers
The Story of the Phoenix Suns
The Story of the Sacramento Kings
The Story of the Washington Wizards

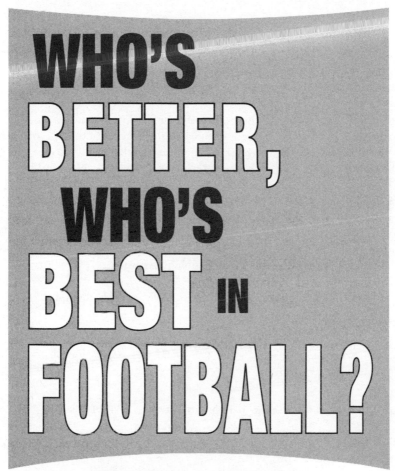

WHO'S BETTER, WHO'S BEST IN FOOTBALL?

Setting the Record Straight on
the Top 65 NFL Players of the Past 65 Years

STEVE SILVERMAN

SPORTS
PUBLISHING

Sports Publishing books may be purchased in bulk at special discounts for sales promotion, corporate gifts, fund-raising, or educational purposes. Special editions can also be created to specifications. For details, contact the Special Sales Department, Sports Publishing, 307 West 36th Street, 11th Floor, New York, NY 10018 or sportspubbooks@skyhorsepublishing.com.

Sports Publishing® is a registered trademark of Skyhorse Publishing, Inc.®, a Delaware corporation.

Visit our website at www.sportspubbooks.com.

10 9 8 7 6 5 4 3 2 1

Library of Congress Cataloging-in-Publication Data is available on file.

Cover design by Tom Lau
Cover photos credit AP Images

Print ISBN: 978-1-61321-726-9
Ebook ISBN: 978-1-61321-753-5

Printed in the United States of America

To my children, Samantha and Gregory, with much love:
May both of you always follow your own dreams.

With love to my sister, Judy, and my uncle, Eddie.

Mom and Dad, both long gone, but always in my heart.

CONTENTS

Contents

INTRODUCTION

I know what you're thinking. As you have picked up this book that purports to rank the top 65 National Football League players of the past 65 years, you are beginning to wonder: "Where do you get off ranking the best players of the past 60 years? What gives you the right?"

Ok, you've gotten it out of your system and it's a fair question to ask. The ranking of players is largely a subjective activity even when objective criteria like yardage, points, and championships are considered. I have tried to give you a definitive list, but it is OK to disagree with my decisions. I can't expect most readers to be in complete agreement especially when the debate between No. 65 and 66 was a long and hard one—even though I had to make both arguments myself.

I have covered the NFL through my entire adult life. I started covering the NFL in 1981, saw Lawrence Taylor practice and play as a rookie, and learned how hard a hitter he was by standing just a few feet away when he made contact with a ball carrier in practice. Although he was still in the first month of his career, I had no doubts that the New York Giants had found a special player.

I have been lucky enough to see and talk to most of the players on the list in person at one point or another in my career. I have also had the opportunity to talk to their coaches and get their opinions on what made these players so special. So as I have ranked these players I have tried to back those rankings with the valued thoughts of those who have played or made their living in the game for many years.

But more than that, I have tried to back those rankings with facts: Notes about players achievements, information about who they played with and what those teammates accomplished, and things that players had to overcome in their careers.

My rankings are based on achievement first and foremost. Joe Montana and Jim Brown are at the top of the list and Jerry Rice follows right behind. All three of these men did more to help their team win games than any players before or since.

Montana and Rice were coached by Bill Walsh, a man who recognized that both had brilliant talent even when others let it pass. Montana was a third-round pick from Notre Dame in 1979 and while Rice was a first-round selection in 1985 from Mississippi Valley State, he wasn't taken until the 16th pick. Walsh himself never knew a thing about Rice until the 1984 season, when he took his 49ers into Houston to play the Oilers in a midseason game. The night before the teams met in the Astrodome, Walsh was watching the sports in his hotel room and that's when he first became familiar with Rice. He had led Mississippi Valley State to a victory that day, running all over the field after making a series of circus catches. Walsh noticed that each of the catches had been difficult to make and that the receiver simply would run away from defenders after he made the catch. He knew he was looking at something special and further study only confirmed his initial analysis.

Walsh was questioned and criticized for taking a receiver from such a small school so early in the draft. But he wasn't interested in winning good grades on Draft Day. He wanted to win games on Sundays and championships in January

The great players each have their own unique style. Montana didn't copy anybody, and neither did Brown or Rice. They followed their own instincts. All the players in this top 65 had their own way of doing things. Perhaps Emmitt Smith borrowed a stiff arm from Walter Payton, or Steve Young took a little bit of his ability to run away from a tackler from Fran Tarkenton's improvisational ability, but these were all their own men.

I have looked for greatness and originality and sought confirmation through the numbers they achieved. I have given them their due and encourage you to read and digest my list. Is it written in stone? No, but it is written in black and white and I stand by my conclusions.

—Steve Silverman

THE PIONEERS:
THE BEST 20 NFL PLAYERS
FROM 1920 TO 1959

Because it is nearly impossible to compare players from different eras, I have narrowed the focus of this book to players from the past 65 years (1948–2013), or what I'll loosely term the Modern Era. But that doesn't mean the players who preceded them don't deserve mention in this book.

Here is a list of the 20 best NFL players from 1920 to 1959. There are 11 years of overlap with the book's master list, which means a few of the players in the chapters that follow had careers that span both eras. There's even one player (Otto Graham) who makes both lists.

The Pioneers: The Best 20 NFL Players from 1920 to 1959

1. Otto Graham, quarterback
2. Sammy Baugh, quarterback
3. Sid Luckman, quarterback
4. Don Hutson, receiver
5. Red Grange, halfback
6. Jim Thorpe, back
7. Cal Hubbard, offensive lineman
8. Mel Hein, center
9. Emlen Tunnell, defensive back
10. Marion Motley, fullback
11. Steve Van Buren, halfback
12. Gino Marchetti, defensive end
13. Andy Robustelli, defensive end
14. Bronko Nagurski, halfback
15. Paddy Driscoll, quarterback
16. Elroy Hirsch, wide receiver
17. Bobby Layne, quarterback
18. Bob Waterfield, quarterback
19. Pete Pihos, tight end
20. Roosevelt Brown, offensive lineman

#1

JIM BROWN

Few things are certain in the world of sports arguments, but when it comes to production by a running back, the vast majority of fans agree that there has never been anyone quite like Jim Brown. My guess is that nobody ever will come close to matching his production over the course of a career. Brown did it all in just nine seasons with the Cleveland Browns and probably could have played another six years if he had been so inclined. However, he retired when he was at or near the peak of his capabilities so he could make movies in Hollywood—and make the cash that was not available in the NFL at the time.

How good was Brown? To the fans who watched from the stands or on television, he was a wrecking ball of a runner who closed out his career by running for 1,863 yards in 1963, 1,446 yards in '64, and 1,544 yards in '65. This was in the days when the league played a 14-game schedule, as opposed to the 16-game schedule they play today. To those who paid their money to see him play, Brown seemed to be a man among boys—quite simply the biggest, strongest and fastest man on the field

Those who were out on the field with him saw basically the same thing as those in the stands. That includes the fellow Hall of Famers who were tasked with bringing him down. Sam Huff, a Hall of Fame linebacker with the New York Giants and Washington Redskins, has spent a good portion of his post-football career talking about Brown's talent. It is a subject that time has not diminished over the years. Huff, who has spent many years in the Washington broadcast booth, has never seen a back who was better or who even approached everything Brown could do on a football field.

"There have been backs who may have been quicker or faster and there are backs who have been bigger, but when you combine speed, strength, quickness, ability and desire, I don't think there's ever been anyone who was close to what Jim Brown could do when he was at his peak," Huff said. "That peak was basically the whole of his career. I don't remember him being slower near the end of his run or weaker. He was the most punishing player I have ever run across. I talked about desire a minute ago. I don't know that his desire was about getting the extra yard or getting into the end zone. It was the desire to beat the man on the other side of the line of scrimmage. Jim played like he wanted to destroy your will. He would simply hurt you when he ran over you and that made it harder each time you had to face him."

"My arms were my weapons," Brown explained. "If you tried to tackle me high, I would use my arms to change your mind. If you tried to tackle me low, that was your choice. It didn't usually work out so well.

"To stop me you would have had to get the best of me mentally. You would have had to make me fear you. That never happened and there was never that much pressure that could have been brought on me. That's how I was able to assert my will."

Brown was a four-time league MVP and also led the NFL in rushing in eight of his nine seasons. He averaged better than 100 yards per game (104) throughout the whole of his career, a record that stands to this day. He also never missed a game during his career due to illness, injury, or anything else. He averaged 5.2 yards per rush throughout his career even though the NFL average for nearly 50 years has been 4.0 yards per carry.

Brown accomplished all of this at a time when running the football really was the key to succeeding in the NFL, or at least it was a bigger part of the picture than it has been in the last 25 years. Coaches will still get in front of microphones today and tell you they must run the ball and stop the run in order to win and do it with a straight face. Ask Pittsburgh head coach Mike Tomlin how important running was in the Steelers' last-minute drive to win Super Bowl XLIII. But when Brown played, a team that could run and stop the run had a great chance to win the title.

Defenses were stacked to stop him. Linebackers like Huff had no other assignment but to stop Brown and still couldn't do it. He went over the 100-yard mark in nearly half the games he played in.

And then he left. Walking away after the 1965 season as the leading rusher in NFL history, his record 12,312 yards stood until Walter Payton surpassed the mark 19 years later. No disrespect to Payton (you'll see him at No. 5 on this list), but as complete a player as he was, it took Payton 435 more carries than Brown to reach that mark.

Brown never had any major regrets about leaving the game early and pursue his acting career, either. "To leave at twenty-nine years old, MVP, having won the championship in '64 and played for it in '65. To go into the movies and break the color barrier and be in a sex scene with Raquel Welch. To get to be in *The Dirty Dozen* with some great actors. To make more money in one year than you damn near made in nine years of football. Everything about it was ingenious," Brown told *Esquire* magazine in 2008.

Those that had to tackle Brown for a living were equally as regret-free that the Cleveland running back said goodbye to the game when he did. But the same cannot be said of the fans of the game that never had enough of watching the greatest running back in football history do what he did best. He played fearlessly and he did it in a way that put the fear of God in others. He falls just short of Joe Montana because he won only one title and could not take over a game in the crucial moments the way the quarterback could.

#2

JERRY RICE

Jerry Rice is largely considered the best wide receiver to ever take the field in the NFL and many believe that he is the best player—regardless of position—to ever line up in league history.

Nevertheless, Rice was merely another name on the draft board in 1985.

Give him credit. Rice had played at Mississippi Valley State and few fans had ever seen him play a college game. Nevertheless, Rice was expected to be a first-round draft pick and nobody was a bigger supporter than Bill Walsh.

The legendary San Francisco head coach first started thinking about Rice in October 1984 when his 49ers were in Houston preparing to play the Oilers the next day. Walsh was watching the sports report on TV and Rice was coming off a game in which he scored five touchdowns, all on plays of 50 yards or more. Then Walsh saw the films and fell in love. "When I saw Rice, I thought immediately of how well he would fit into our offense," Walsh said later, "and how he would give us an extra dimension."

That's what separated Walsh from other game-planners and talent scouts. His bold assessment allowed him to throw the inexperienced Rice right into the mix without hesitation. Other coaches would have worked him in slowly.

The 49ers were able to select Rice with the No. 16 pick in the draft. Walsh never though he would get that lucky. He thought Rice would go within the first five picks of the draft and was thrilled at the chance to get him. A number of 49ers scouts thought Walsh had gone off the deep end and that Rice was worth no more than a sixth-round choice. Rice had played at a Division I-AA school and he didn't have the 4.3 speed that makes scouts' jaws drop. Walsh didn't care because he knew Rice had football speed if not stop-watch speed.

In San Francisco, Rice became an immediate weapon. While he dropped some balls as a rookie that he would never drop again, Rice's ability to deliver the big play showed up in Week 14 when he caught 10 passes for 241 yards in a game against the Los Angeles Rams. He never looked back. In his second season, Rice caught 86 passes for 1,570 yards and 15 touchdowns and was arguably the best receiver in the league. Those great numbers didn't prevent him from fumbling away a sure touchdown while running in the open field after the catch in a playoff game against the New York Giants, though.

The argument came to an abrupt end the following year. In the 1987 season that had been torn apart by a players' strike, Rice caught 65 passes for 1,078 yards and 22 touchdowns in only 12 games.

The numbers continued to build up and so did Rice's monumental achievements. Rice was at his absolute best in Super Bowl XXIII against the Cincinnati Bengals, the only Super Bowl that Joe Montana played in that he didn't win the game's MVP The award instead went to Rice, who caught 11 passes for 215 yards and a touchdown. More than the numbers, Rice made key catches on the game-winning drive in the final moments. One of those was a second-and-20 play from the Cincinnati 45 after center Randy Cross had been penalized for going downfield to sustain one of his pass blocks. Rice ran a square-in route over the middle and even though the Bengals attempted to cover him with three men—Lewis Billups, David Fulcher, and Ray Horton—Rice got free. Montana's pass hit him in stride and he ran the ball another 14 yards after catching it for a 27-yard gain.

Walsh had his opponent right where he wanted. He knew the Bengals would sell out to stop Rice, so a play was called for Roger Craig and John Taylor. Craig couldn't get free from the linebacker on "20 Halfback Curl X Up" but Taylor found the seam and Montana hit him in the end zone for the game-winning score.

"It was just a great moment," said Rice. "I didn't make that catch but it felt just like I did. To see your teammate succeed and to know that you played a huge role in making that happen was just a wonderful feeling. I couldn't have been any happier if I had made the catch."

A strong argument can be made that Rice cemented his status and made his case to be immortalized on the Mount Rushmore of sports (if such a monument existed) along with Babe Ruth, Michael Jordan, and Bobby Orr for his performance during the three-year span from 1994 through 1996. Rice caught 342 passes during those three seasons for 4,601 yards and 36 touchdowns. That three-year average of 114–1,534–12 meant that Rice was simply an uncoverable receiver who could get free any time he wanted.

It was Rice's unshakable desire to get the most out of his ability and his unquenchable thirst to be the best player possible that kept him performing at a top level throughout his career. "I wanted to be the best and I wanted to separate myself from anyone else who played the position," Rice said. "I wanted to play knowing that I had given my best on every play I took the field. I didn't want to waste any opportunity. It was the game within a game. People tell you how much you are doing or how great you are and you can't let that satisfy you at any point. The minute you start to believe what people are saying is the minute you start to relax. That can never be allowed to happen."

Rice got his career going with Montana as his quarterback and then spent the latter half of his 49ers career with Steve Young calling signals. While Rice was in the Montana camp and threw his support behind Joe during his battle with Young for the quarterback job, Rice eventually caught more touchdown passes from Young than any other quarterback.

"It was the best feeling in the world to know that Jerry was out there with you," Young said. "When we took the field in Super Bowl XXIX [against San Diego], everyone in a Niner uniform had this feeling of unbelievable confidence that we were going to win and we were the better team," Young said. "It worked out that way as we jumped out to a big lead and won fairly comfortably [49–26]. The reason most of us felt confident was that we could look over there in the locker room and see Jerry getting ready and preparing for the game. He was the best player in the game and he was lining up for us. That's all we needed to know."

Rice's career would finish up in a Seattle Seahawks uniform after a relatively successful stint with the Oakland Raiders following 16 seasons in San Francisco. His last season was 2004, and his numbers suggest that he may have stayed a year too long. However, he was the best at his craft for at least 15 years of his 20-year career and he is the standard all other receivers will be measured by for the next generation. He is the only player in league history with 200 touchdowns, finishing his career with 208 total, 197 of which came as a receiver.

Jerry Rice

LEADING RECEIVERS, BY YARDS					
Player	Years	Yards	RPG	YPG	TDs per game
1. Jerry Rice	1985-2004	22,895	5.1	75.6	0.65
2. Terrell Owens	1996-2010	15,934	4.9	72.8	0.48
3. Randy Moss	1998-2012	15,292	4.5	70.1	0.72
4. Isaac Bruce	1994-2009	15,208	4.6	68.2	0.41
5. Tony Gonzalez	1997-2013	15,127	4.9	56	0.29
6. Tim Brown	1988-2004	14,934	4.3	58.6	0.49
7. Marvin Harrison	1996-2008	14,580	5.8	76.7	0.42
8. James Lofton	1978-1993	14,004	3.3	60.1	0.32
9. Cris Carter	1987-2002	13,899	4.7	59.4	0.62
10. Henry Ellard	1983-1999	13,777	3.6	60.4	0.29

#3

JOE MONTANA

It's not a popularity contest and it's not about who most looked the part. Even though those are both areas in which Joe Montana acquitted himself very well, they are beside the point.

It comes down to this: Quarterback is the most important position position in football. The most important thing a quarterback does is throw the football. Montana threw the football with as much accuracy and consistency as any quarterback who ever played the game—even if he was not known for his arm strength.

His admirers are cross-generational. Quarterbacks who came before Montana never raise the issue that things would have been different if he had played in an era when defensive ends like Deacon

Jones used to batter quarterbacks with his helmet and that it was far more physical in the 1960s and '70s than it was in the Montana era. Conversely, top quarterbacks of the present day like Tom Brady and Peyton Manning frequently name Montana when it's time to talk about the quarterback they admire the most.

Montana was a brilliant passer who threw for 300 or more yards in a game 39 times in his career and won the important game nearly every time he stepped out on the field. He specialized in the comeback win, registering 31 fourth-quarter, come-from-behind victories during his career.

His coach and mentor, the late Bill Walsh, molded Montana into a quarterback who understood the game and who knew what it took to win in the fourth quarter, but Walsh never took too much credit when it came to Montana's ability to perform in the clutch. "He had this amazing confidence that he was going to deliver," Walsh said. "It's the kind of thing a lot of athletes like to talk about and will do their best to project, but many of them don't really have the confidence that they need to in order to succeed regularly. Joe always did. He wanted the opportunity to succeed when it was all out in front of him and he flourished in that environment. It was where he wanted to be and that's when he always did his best work."

The ability to play it cool allowed Montana to lead the San Francisco 49ers to victories in four Super Bowl appearances. There was never even a hint of nervousness about his own talent or his team's ability to come through with the game on the line. Montana never allowed himself to fall into those traps. He had the utmost confidence in himself and he certainly believed in the talents of offensive weapons Jerry Rice, Dwight Clark, Roger Craig as well as the Niner defense to get the job done.

"As far as I was concerned you would go over things in your mind," Montana explained before the Niners won their fourth Super Bowl after the 1989 season against the Denver Broncos. "I went down the checklist. I believed in what we were trying to do. So from that point on, it became a matter of executing what we were trying to do as a team. I wanted to execute to the best of my ability. Make the best read I could, make the best throw I could and then keep on doing it."

Montana set the stage for a career of amazing performances with everything on the line in the closing moments of the 1981 NFC Championship Game against the Dallas Cowboys. The Cowboys were "America's Team" back then and they were in the business of squashing dreams. Dallas had the Niners on the ropes, and it all appeared to be coming to an end. Down six points with 58 seconds to go, Montana took the snap from the Dallas 6-yard line. As he rolled right, the 6-foot-9 Ed "Too Tall" Jones closed in on Montana and the sidelines, threatening to swallow him up and end both the play and the Niners' season. Backing up to avoid the rush, Montana pump-faked, causing Jones to jump prematurely. This presented Montana with a passing lane at the Dallas 14-yard line to put the ball in a place where only the high-jumping Clark could catch it. Clark's catch over defensive back Everson Walls in the back corner of the end zone won the conference championship for the 49ers and forever changed the legacy of the franchise. It has since been known, simply, as "The Catch."

The 49ers had been mere bit players before Montana came along. They had some nice years with John Brodie at quarterback in the 1960s and with Dick Nolan at head coach, but the 49ers were never considered with the elite of the NFL. Opponents? Sure. Upstarts? Perhaps. Contenders? No way. Montana, with the help of Walsh and a few key teammates, built the 49ers into one of the greatest teams of all time.

There was nothing Montana was unable to pull off when he had the ball in his hands at the end of a game. He was intently competitive and undeniably successful. If he had the best team, he would slaughter you, as he exhibited in Super Bowl XIX against the Miami Dolphins and Super Bowl XXIV against the Broncos, the latter a 45-point rout. If his opponent was as good or better than his club, Montana would simply find a way to beat them, as he did twice in Super Bowl wins over the Cincinnati Bengals (Super Bowls XVI and XXIII), Montana was helped dramatically in his final two Super Bowl wins by the presence of Jerry Rice, the greatest receiver in pro-football history. The Niners also had an outstanding defense that never received proper credit because it was overshadowed by the team's offensive stars and head coach Bill Walsh.

Montana's legacy will live on. If there is one man on this planet who has the inherent right to resent Montana, it is Steve Young, who ultimately succeeded Montana as the quarterback of the 49ers. Montana never rolled out the welcome mat for Young and in many ways made life miserable for him by giving the gregarious Young the cold shoulder at every opportunity and never allowing him to feel like anything but an intruder. The passage of time makes that understandable because Montana was so intently competitive that he wanted to hold the job he loved for as a long as he could. But Young, brilliant and deserving of a spot on this list in his own right (as No. 58), never allowed his judgment of Montana to be clouded by personal slights. As he readied to give postgame analysis following the Pittsburgh Steelers' victory over the Arizona Cardinals in Super Bowl XLIII, Young marveled at Ben Roethlisberger's late drive. "Look at what Ben is doing," Young said. "It's Montana-esque. It's just amazing."

Montana's big-game performances have proven to be gems. They have not dimmed as the years have gone by. Instead they have become polished and their luster is even brighter as time has passed than they were when they were so brilliantly composed.

UNDEFEATED QUARTERBACKS WITH MULTIPLE SUPER BOWL WINS

1. Joe Montana, San Francisco 49ers

Super Bowl	Comp.	Att.	Pct.	Yds.	TD	Int.	Ps Rtg	Result (opponent)
XVI	14	22	63.6	157	1	0	100.0	W 26-21 (Cincinnati)
XIX	24	35	68.6	331	3	0	127.2	W 38-16 (Miami)
XXIII	23	36	63.9	357	2	0	115.2	W 20-16 (Cincinnati)
XXIV	22	29	75.9	297	5	0	147.6	W 55-10 (Denver)
TOTALS	**83**	**122**	**68.0**	**1,142**	**11**	**0**	**127.8**	**4-0**

2. Jim Plunkett, Oakland Raiders

Super Bowl	Comp.	Att.	Pct.	Yds.	TD	Int.	Ps Rtg	Result (opponent)
XV	13	21	61.9	261	3	0	145.0	W 27-10 (Philadelphia)
XVIII	16	25	64.0	172	1	0	97.4	W 38-9 (Washington)
TOTALS	**29**	**46**	**63.0**	**433**	**4**	**0**	**122.8**	**2-0**

3. Terry Bradshaw, Pittsburgh Steelers

Super Bowl	Comp.	Att.	Pct.	Yds.	TD	Int.	Ps Rtg	Result (opponent)
IX	9	14	64.3	96	1	0	108.0	W 16-6 (Minnesota)
X	9	19	47.4	209	2	0	122.5	W 21-17 (Dallas)
XIII	17	30	56.7	318	4	1	119.2	W 35-31 (Dallas)
XIV	14	21	66.7	309	2	3	101.9	W 31-19 (L.A. Rams)
TOTALS	**49**	**84**	**58.3**	**932**	**9**	**4**	**112.8**	**4-0**

4. Troy Aikman, Dallas

Super Bowl	Comp.	Att.	Pct.	Yds.	TD	Int.	Ps Rtg	Result (opponent)
XXVII	22	30	73.3	273	4	0	140.7	W 52-17 (Buffalo)
XXVIII	19	27	70.4	207	0	1 7	7.2	W 30-13 (Buffalo)
XXX	15	23	65.2	209	1	0	108.8	W 27-17 (Pittsburgh)
TOTALS	**56**	**80**	**70.0**	**689**	**5**	**1**	**111.9**	**3-0**

5. Bart Starr, Green Bay

Super Bowl	Comp.	Att.	Pct.	Yds.	TD	Int.	Ps Rtg	Result (opponent)
I	16	23	69.6	250	2	1	116.2	W 35-10 (Kansas City)
II	13	24	54.2	202	1	0	96.2	W 33-14 (Oakland)
TOTALS	**29**	**47**	**61.7**	**452**	**3**	**1**	**106.0**	**2-0**

#4

LAWRENCE TAYLOR

More than any other individual, Taylor gets credit for turning around the New York Giants franchise. From the time he arrived in New York prior to the 1981 season, Taylor was all about committing mayhem on the field. Giants head coach Ray Perkins had a team on his hands that had not seen any postseason play since the 1963 NFL Championship Game against the Chicago Bears, and the Giants had been punching bags for much of the ensuing 18 years.

That changed immediately with the arrival of Taylor. Instead of absorbing the blows, the Giants started delivering them. It wasn't all Taylor's doing, as a young defense started to come of age and the Giants also had the key elements of a resilient offense with Phil Simms at quarterback and a competent running game, but it was the ferocious Taylor who was the first item up for discussion when opponents started game-planning against New York.

Taylor redefined the outside linebacker position in the Giants' 3–4 defense. He could chase any play down from behind with his remarkable speed and was at his best when he was in pursuit of the quarterback. The Giants' defense, which ranked 24th in total yards allowed in 1980 improved to third with Taylor in the lineup. Opponents had scored 425 points against New York in 1980; that total dipped to 257 in 1981.

Taylor, who unofficially recorded 9.5 sacks in his rookie season, had a natural leverage when coming around the corner to get the quarterbacks. His first position coach in the NFL was Bill Parcells, who served as the Giants' linebacker coach in his rookie season. Parcells had some influence on Taylor in terms of his on-field positioning in the defensive scheme, but he never had to do a thing in terms of technique when Taylor was rushing the passer, or in terms of passion when L.T. was playing the game. The same holds for Bill Belichick, who was the Giants' defensive coordinator during the prime of Taylor's career (after Parcells was named head coach).

Belichick, who would later earn his own spurs as one of the top five head coaches in NFL history with the New England Patriots, said that Taylor's recklessness with his body on the field is unparalleled in football history. It also served as the benchmark for the level of commitment he demanded from his teammates.

A 10-time Pro Bowler and eight-time first-team All-Pro selection, Taylor won the Defensive Player of the Year award three times during his career (the only player in league history to win it more than twice). Taylor was at his most dominant during the 1986 season when he became only the second defensive player in history to capture league-wide MVP honors. He had 20.5 sacks that season and was virtually unstoppable even though Giants opponents went to unprecedented lengths to stop him.

Hall of Fame coach Bill Walsh was so fearful of Taylor's ability to chase plays down from behind that he never ran away from him. Instead, when the 49ers decided to run the ball against the Giants, it was directly at Taylor where one or two blockers might be able to control Taylor long enough to give a running back just enough of a crack to get past him. That was impossible when Taylor was in full flight running a play down from the opposite side.

Washington Redskins coach Joe Gibbs had seen Taylor end quarterback Joe Theismann's career during the 1985 season by breaking his leg after he came around the corner to sack him in a Monday night game. The gruesome scene lives on nearly 25 years later as a YouTube staple and pushed Gibbs to invent the H-back position, which was designed to keep an extra blocker in just to slow Taylor down.

The Theismann incident both dogged and exaggerated Taylor's reputation throughout his career. As much as he wanted to get to the quarterback when he was on the field, he didn't want to maim them. As soon as Theismann went down, Taylor started motioning for Washington's medical staff to come out onto the field to attend to the fallen quarterback.

As far as his own injuries were concerned, Taylor often paid them no heed. He played with a hairline fracture in his tibia in 1987 and a broken foot in 1989. Giants trainers once had to steal his helmet to keep him from returning to the field after he suffered a concussion. In a legendary game against the New Orleans Saints in the 1988 season, Taylor played despite torn shoulder ligaments and a torn pectoral muscle that left him short of breath and in constant pain. He stayed in the lineup because teammates Harry Carson, Carl Banks, and quarterback Phil Simms were unable to play. Taylor had seven tackles, three sacks, and two forced fumbles during the game and Giants came away with a 13–12 victory.

Hall of Fame coach and broadcaster John Madden said he never saw a defensive player who could come close to matching Taylor's on-field ferocity and whose all-around impact was to change the way the game was played. "Nobody changed defense more than Lawrence Taylor," Madden told ESPN. "He changed the way linebackers play. He changed the way teams rush the passer. He changed the way linebackers play and he changed the way offenses block linebackers."

Former Philadelphia Eagles quarterback Ron Jaworski's obsession with knowing where Taylor was on the field has not been exaggerated. Jaworski was one of the top quarterbacks in the game and led the Eagles to an appearance in Super Bowl XV against the Oakland Raiders, but from the moment Taylor entered the league the next season he appeared to live in Philadelphia's backfield whenever the two teams played. "I looked for him before every snap," Jaworski said. "It was a matter of trying to survive."

Taylor's obsession with getting to the passer allowed him to register 142 sacks for his career (including the unofficial 9.5 from his rookie season) and there were times that he might have missed some of his other responsibilities because of his desire to get to the quarterback. As great as Taylor was, his off-the-field recklessness may have kept him from being an even more dominant player. He was troubled by alcohol and drug abuse throughout his career as his passion for hard living was nearly as great as his desire to wreak havoc on the field. He developed a reputation for maniacal behavior with every step he took and that had to have some impact of his on-field production.

Taylor was suspended four games for his drug use in 1988 but managed to avoid another suspension throughout the rest of his career. He retired at the end of the 1993 season and then went into rehab twice for cocaine use in 1995. He would ultimately learn to live his life without the substance and have a career in film and another obsession—golf. But his dominance on the field turned the Giants franchise around and allowed him to reinvent the way defense is played.

#5

WALTER PAYTON

They called him "Sweetness" because of his personality. But Walter Payton's production made him more of a throwback than any other football player of his era. When Payton was drafted by the Chicago Bears out of Jackson State in 1975, it was before specialization had set in around the league. There weren't first-down run stuffers and third-down pass rushers. Instead, there were defensive linemen who were expected to play every down. Defensive backs were expected to cover the pass and stop the run. Perhaps an extra defensive back was thrown into the mix in the fourth quarter to prevent a big pass play.

But you had to play the game the whole way. Payton played a complete game. He ran like a terror, blocked like a warrior, caught passes as if he were a wideout, and threw the ball for accuracy and distance whenever the coaching staff asked him to.

He surpassed Jim Brown as the game's all-time leading rusher during the 1984 season. He finished his career with 16,726 yards in 13 seasons. He punished tacklers throughout his run in the NFL even though he was 5-foot-10 and his playing weight was only 200 pounds. He missed one game in his rookie season and he never missed another. On a team that many recognize as having had the greatest single season in the history of football, Payton was the best all-around player on the 1985 Bears.

Mike Ditka, the head coach of those Bears and the franchise's icon since the death of George Halas in 1983, called Payton the greatest football player he's ever seen. "I never saw a player who gave more of himself on every play he was out there than Walter Payton," Ditka said. "There wasn't anything he couldn't do in a dominant fashion. He was the best runner, the best blocker and the best receiver. He could throw it when you wanted him to and he would do anything he could to help his team win. What more can you ask?"

In a league in which many of the best players have a hard time sustaining performances from one year to the next, Payton would not allow himself to go into a slump or ever be satisfied. That's why he had 77 games with more then 100 yards rushing, including a 275-yard effort in one game against the Minnesota Vikings. He rushed for more than 1,000 yards in a season 10 times, an NFL record at the time of his retirement, and was voted to the Pro Bowl nine times.

No one who played for the Bears ever caught more passes than Payton's 492. In fact, no one even came close. No Hall of Fame running back ever blocked with as much gusto as Payton, who routinely put linebackers and defensive linemen on their backs by taking them out at the knees before they could get near his quarterback.

Playing with some mediocre teams in the mid 1970s and early '80s, Payton broke hundreds of tackles just to get back to the line of scrimmage. Defenses were aware that some of those Bears teams possessed no threat other than Payton, so they made stopping him the focus of their game plan.

That's part of the reason that of the 11 passes he completed on the halfback option play, eight went for touchdowns. The other reason is that the second most prolific ground gainer in NFL history had a stronger arm than a lot of the quarterbacks he played with over the years.

At one point, when injuries decimated Chicago's quarterback position, Payton took a few snaps behind center. He could've handled the kicking and punting duties, too, if necessary. He did at Jackson State, where he kicked five field goals and 54 extra points and had a 39-yard punting average.

"I got as much pleasure watching him block somebody as watching him run for a touchdown," Ditka said. "Or watching him catch a pass or throw a pass or kick the ball. He could do it all. In practice he did it as well as most people. He was just a talented guy. He was also the hardest-working guy we had. He was the first guy there and the last guy to leave.

"He came to camp in the best shape of anybody that I've ever seen and he did it all on his own. He ran the hills, he lifted weights, he ran constantly up and down. He was a machine."

Payton's offseason conditioning program may have been the key to his consistent production. While others used training camp to get in shape, Payton would run hills in order to prepare for training camp; once he got there, it was a breeze for him. Payton started running up a 92-foot hill in an Arlington Heights, Illinois, landfill as many as 20 times a day. That training regimen built up his legs and endurance to a point that shocked his teammates.

"I saw what he was doing and I couldn't believe it," said former Bears fullback Matt Suhey. "It was the most grueling and painful thing I ever saw yet he never complained. Nobody else could do it and keep doing it like Walter. He was driven to be the best he could be."

Payton was extremely effective during the 1985 season, rushing for 1,551 yards and averaging 4.8 yards per carry, the second-best total of his career. (He averaged 5.5 yards per carry in 1977 when he ran for a career-best 1,852 yards, the third-highest total ever in a 14-game season.) The '85 Bears rolled to a 15–1 record and crushed the New York Giants, Los Angeles Rams, and New England Patriots and captured the franchise's only Super Bowl.

Payton's all-around talent and professionalism were on display throughout the season, but never more so than in the Week Three, 33–24 win at Minnesota. With the Bears trailing the Vikings late in the game, Jim McMahon came off the bench to get the passing game going. As Willie Gault ran deep, Payton delivered a crushing block on the blitz that allowed McMahon to throw a touchdown pass. When the Bears finally lost later that season to the Miami Dolphins and the focus of the undefeated season was gone, it was Payton who got them back on track against the Indianapolis Colts the following week with a 111-yard rushing effort.

Payton was the picture of vigor and health throughout his career; that made his 1999 death due to liver disease all the more tragic. Payton's career rushing record has since been broken by Emmitt Smith, but his legacy as a complete player will never be touched.

#6

JOHNNY UNITAS

He is the standard that all other quarterbacks have in their minds. Johnny Unitas—Johnny U. to a generation of football fans—was the first of the great quarterbacks in the game's modern era. Otto Graham was a tremendous winner and Bobby Layne commanded the huddle at least as well as Unitas, but when it came to throwing the football and putting it exactly where he wanted it to go, nobody who came before him could match Johnny Unitas.

His statistics will not match those of Peyton Manning and Tom Brady in today's pass-happy era, but Unitas played when teams really did try to run the ball and balance in the offense meant mixing long runs with short ones to dominate games.

Johnny Unitas

Unitas was the quarterback who changed the game. Weeb Ewbank, his first head coach in Baltimore, recognized how strong and accurate Unitas's arm was. So did Colts wide receiver Raymond Berry, a glue-fingered type who spent hour after hour running precise patterns that both he and Unitas knew in their sleep. When Berry was running a square out, Unitas did not even have to look at the receiver. He knew that when he completed his dropback, all he had to do was take one step and fire the ball to the sidelines 12 yards ahead and Berry would be there at the time the ball arrived.

Unitas was the best quarterback in the NFL and perhaps the key to its growth—leading the Colts to the NFL championship over the New York Giants in the 1958 title game in what became known as "The Greatest Game Ever Played." Unitas was the standard bearer for all the future quarterbacks who hailed from a football hotbed called western Pennsylvania. Everyone there wanted to follow Unitas, who was born in Pittsburgh in 1933. Western Pennsylvanians Joe Namath, Joe Montana, Dan Marino, and Jim Kelly all became legends and all patterned their games after what Unitas did. All four followed Unitas in the Hall of Fame.

Unitas was also a prolific passer for his era. He led the NFL in passing yardage four times between 1957 and 1963 and led the league in touchdowns four straight times between 1957 and 1960. But when you lead the league with 3,099 yards and 25 touchdown passes, it doesn't quite get the point across. Those were outstanding numbers for the crew-cut era but they're middle-of-the-road numbers in the new millennium.

While his talent was unprecedented, what made Unitas so special to his teammates was his toughness. Unitas was a pocket passer for the Colts from the moment he first tied his high-top shoes. He would wait until the last possible instant to get rid of the football and if he had to take punishment in order to wait for Berry or Lenny Moore to get open, Unitas did. He never opened his mouth about it.

"I'll never forget the shots this guy would take in order to throw a pass," said former Colts defensive lineman Art Donovan. "It was awful. This guy would get hammered out there just about every game and sometimes it seemed like he would get hit on every play. But nothing ever changed. He would stand in there and take it and he would not complain. He had to be the toughest Colt of them all because he took so much punishment."

Most of Unitas's records have long been erased from the NFL record book. For example, when Unitas was done playing following the 1973 season (which he spent in a San Diego Chargers uniform), he had thrown for 300 or more yards a record 27 times in a game. That record now belongs to Marino, who did it a whopping 63 times with the Miami Dolphins.

However, Unitas still ranks in the top spot for most consecutive games with at least one touchdown pass. He did it 47 times between 1956 and 1960, something that Brett Favre managed to do 36 times between 2002 and 2004. One of the reasons that Unitas was able to set that mark is that it never mattered to him that much. Yardage, touchdowns, completions, and attempts were just numbers to him. The only thing he was interested in was winning the game. If he could have played a game just handing off and the Colts had scored nothing but touchdowns, he would have been happy to do just that. Many quarterbacks will tell the media that personal glory means nothing to them, but they are telling bold-faced lies.

"I never paid much attention to the touchdown streak, not like the newspaper people and radio people did," he told the *Baltimore Sun*. "My whole thing was to just win games, using everything at my disposal. It didn't matter if we did it by running or throwing, as long as our concentration was on winning. Everyone was on the same page. There were no jealousies among anyone. The team ran the plays I called and never questioned them."

At the end of his career and in the ensuing years, Unitas did not like what he saw on the football field. He did not like the proliferation of coaches and watching quarterbacks who no longer called their own plays. "Who knows more about what's going on in the game than the quarterback?" Unitas asked. "That's why the quarterback should be calling plays. To think that an assistant coach knows better about what will work on the field is ridiculous. They're just trying to justify themselves. I want the quarterback to call his own plays."

Unitas's top rival during pro football's prime growth years in the early 1960s was Bart Starr of the Green Bay Packers. While Starr never had the numbers that Unitas did, he was at his best when it was all on the line in championship games; Unitas had great respect for Starr's ability to play winning football. Starr was always supremely confident—except when he took the field against Unitas and the Colts. "[Unitas] could do anything he wanted with the football in his hands," Starr said. "He could throw it where he wanted and do it in an instant. When he was on the field the Colts always had a chance to win."

Never mind that Starr won 10 of his last 15 head-to-head encounters with Unitas. He had the superior team. No quarterback ever did more for the game than Unitas, who lifted professional football up on his shoulders and then hurled it into the sports stratosphere.

#7

PEYTON MANNING

Imagine, if you will, that you were the chosen one.

From the time you first stepped into a classroom in seventh grade, you were deemed the best and the brightest of every student in your classroom.

Any time you participated in a class or took a test, you were expected to be the best. It started that day when you were 13 years old—and those expectations never waned.

Now, transfer that to the football field. From the day you first slipped on shoulder pads and donned a helmet, you were expected to be the best. If you were the top player on the field, you merely lived up to expectations. If your team lost the game or you made a mistake, you were a disappointment.

That's the great weight that Peyton Manning has carried with him every step of the way throughout his football career. The son of a great NFL quarterback in Archie Manning, Peyton was a dynamic high school player who was expected to be a star college quarterback.

When he enrolled at the University of Tennessee and disappointed those who wanted him to follow in his father's footsteps at Ole Miss, the pressure became even greater. Manning never bowed to that pressure and was the best passer in Southeastern Conference history.

Everything Manning had done in his career prepared him to be successful in the NFL. He became the first choice in the 1998 draft, and he quickly became the face of the Indianapolis Colts. It took one year for Manning to turn a losing franchise into one of the glamour teams in the league.

The Colts went 3-13 in Manning's rookie year, but they were a 13-3 team by the 1999 season. Manning quickly became one of the most cerebral players in the game, as he knew the game so well that he basically took over nearly all the play-calling duties for the Colts.

Manning's ascension was the result of study and hard work. While he spent many hours on the practice field trying to learn and improve his game, he spent many more hours in the film room, learning his responsibilities, learning what each of his ten teammates was supposed to do on every play, and getting a firm grip on all the options the opposing defense had.

"One of the things I have learned about this game is that the more prepared you are, the better chance you have of achieving success," Manning explained. "You can control how you perform on the field, and when you understand how your opponents are most likely going to try to stop you, you have a much better chance of success.

"I knew that if I was going to be successful, I would have to do all the work I could on the practice field and in the film room."

Manning was clearly one of the most gifted passers in NFL history, but was never willing to rely on his gifts of passing accuracy, a quick release, or his ability to fire the ball down the field. Instead, it was his work at diagnosing what his opponents would do that would allow him to take his talent and rise above the rest.

Manning's record of achievement in Indianapolis was superb, as he never failed to complete less than 62 percent of his passes after his rookie season. His touchdown and yardage totals mounted, and so did his victory totals.

He was remarkable during the 2004 season, when he completed 336-of-497 passes for 4,557 yards with an overwhelming 49 touchdown passes and just 10 interceptions. It seemed that Manning could go out on the field and torch NFL defenses any time he felt like it, as the Colts overwhelmed nearly all their opponents in rolling to a 12-4 record.

The magic continued the following season, as the Colts were even better. They dominated the regular season with a 14-2 mark. However, Manning's regular season success was not accompanied by top performances in the playoffs.

No matter how brilliant his numbers were during the year, Manning tripped up in the postseason. Usually, the New England Patriots were involved, as Manning could not find a way to outscheme Patriots coach Bill Belichick and his brilliant quarterback in Tom Brady. However, Manning also had problems contending with the Pittsburgh Steelers' aggressive defense.

Finally, in the 2006 season, Manning had had enough. The Colts overcame their history of postseason failures as they hammered the Kansas City Chiefs 23-8 in the Wild Card round of the playoffs. Then they went on the road and defeated the hard-hitting Baltimore Ravens 15-8 in the divisional playoffs, which set up another confrontation with the Patriots in the AFC Championship game.

Heartbreak appeared to be the theme of this game for Manning, as the Patriots raced out to a 21-6 halftime lead. But this time,

Manning would not be stopped in the second half. He scored on a short run in the third quarter and then threw a short touchdown pass to little-used Dan Klecko to tie the game.

The Colts would go on to clinch a berth in the Super Bowl by outlasting New England 38-34. Two weeks later, the Colts would earn their only Super Bowl title of the Manning era by beating the Chicago Bears 29-17 in the rain in Miami in Super Bowl XLI.

"Those wins over the Patriots and the Bears meant as much to me as any wins in my career," Manning said. "We had been stopped so many times on the way to the Super Bowl, so beating the Patriots meant we were no longer falling short. Then, to beat the Bears and win the Super Bowl. It's what every player dreamed of and it meant so much to all of us."

The Colts would make a return appearance in Super Bowl XLIV against New Orleans, but they fell to the upstart Saints 31-17.

Eventually, Manning's time in Indianapolis would come to an end, as a degenerative condition in his neck wiped out his 2011 season. The Colts would allow Manning to leave via free agency in the offseason, and the quarterback would eventually sign with the Denver Broncos.

However, success was anything but a guarantee. While Manning passed a physical prior to signing with the Broncos, there were reports that he no longer had the arm strength to throw his signature sideline passes and that he was a shell of his former self.

Then the season started, and it was almost as if Manning had not missed a beat. He was directing the Denver offense with the same skill and rhythm that he had done in his heyday with the Colts.

He threw for 4,659 yards in 2012 with the Broncos, along with 37 touchdowns and just 11 interceptions. That was just a prelude for the 2013 season, when Manning threw for 5,477 yards along with a record 55 touchdown passes and just 10 interceptions.

The Broncos made it to Super Bowl XLVIII against the Seattle Seahawks, but they were unable to bring home the Vince Lombardi Trophy.

Seattle was simply too powerful and quick on the defensive side of the ball, and the explosive Denver offense was smothered in the biggest game.

Manning has dominated NFL regular season games and statistics like no other quarterback in the game's history. He has one Super Bowl triumph to his credit, but his lack of postseason success has been an issue for his critics.

Still, Manning is perhaps the most prolific quarterback the game has ever known, and he is among the most legendary passers in the sport's history.

He has been the best and brightest since his first days with a football, and he has lived up to his enormous potential.

BEST PASSING SEASONS EVER

Rank	QB	Team	Year	Att.	Comp	Pct.	Yards	YPA	TDs	Int	Rtg.
1	Aaron Rodgers	GB	2011	343	502	68.3	4,643	9.2	45	6	122.5
2	Peyton Manning	Ind.	2004	336	497	67.6	4,557	9.2	49	10	121.1
3	Nick Foles	Phil.	2013	203	317	64	2,891	9.1	27	2	119.2
4	Tom Brady	NE	2007	398	578	68.9	4,806	8.3	50	8	117.2
5	Peyton Manning	Den.	2013	450	659	68.3	5,477	8.3	55	10	115.1
6	Steve Young	SF	1994	324	461	70.3	3,969	8.61	35	10	112.8
7	Joe Montana	SF	1989	271	386	70.2	3,521	9.12	26	8	112.4
8	Tom Brady	NE	2010	324	492	65.9	3,900	7.9	36	4	111
5	Daunte Culpepper	Minn.	2004	379	548	69.2	4,717	8.6	39	11	110.9
10	Drew Brees	SD	2004	262	400	65.5	3,159	7.9	27	7	104.8

UNITAS VS. MANNING

	W-L-T	Cmp	Att.	Pct.	Yards	TDs	Int	Rating	YPA
John Unitas	118-64-4	2,830	5,186	54.6	40,239	290	253	78.2	7.8
Peyton Manning	167-73-0	5,532	8,452	65.5	64,964	491	219	97.2	7.7

#8

DEACON JONES

Deacon Jones was so good at rushing the passer that his former coach, George Allen, called him the greatest defensive player of the modern era. Jones was also as inventive in front of the microphone as he was devastating on the field. He invented his nickname of Deacon "because nobody would ever remember a player named David Jones." Jones coined the term sack and the NFL, to its credit, had the good sense to adopt the phrase without adding its own spin to it.

Jones starred for the Los Angels Rams from 1961 through 1971 before closing out the last three years of his career with the San Diego Chargers and the Washington Redskins. He was the pre-eminent defensive player of his time, which is saying something considering he played at the same time as Ray Nitschke, Willie Davis, Dick Butkus, and Larry Wilson. He had devastating speed from the defensive end position which he combined with a concussion-inducing head slap (now outlawed) that often rendered opposing offensive tackles helpless. Then Jones would get after the quarterback and bring him down behind the line of scrimmage.

"I called it sacking the quarterback because it was like war when they would 'sack' the city," Jones explained. "It was just devastating, man. That was my contribution to the game."

The sack would not become an official statistic for the National Football League until the 1982 season, some eight years after Jones last put on a uniform. So, officially, Jones has zero sacks on his NFL resume. But football historian John Turney went back to try and get sack totals on many of the great players who played prior to the era, including the term's inventor. Turney's research, determined through official NFL play-by-play charts and double-checked through NFL Films, found Jones had 173.5 quarterback sacks in his career. That total would be good enough to rank him third all-time in the sack department, behind only Bruce Smith (200) and Reggie White (198).

A case can be made that Jones had the best five-year run of any defensive player in league history. He recorded 106 sacks between 1964 and 1968. The last two years of that run saw Jones record a cool 50 sacks.

He went up against Hall of Fame linemen of the era such as Forrest Gregg of the Green Bay Packers, Jim Parker of the Baltimore Colts, and Bob St. Clair of the San Francisco 49ers, and all of those greats almost always needed help to contend with the speed of Jones. "They all needed help," Jones said. "Nobody could handle me alone. I was just too mean and too bad."

As the years have gone by, Jones is only too happy to answer reporters' questions and he often does so in WWE style as he talks about how great he is. If you listen carefully, Jones has his tongue planted firmly in his cheek and he is almost always having a good time at the expense of his questioner. Jones was a great team player as well a sack specialist and he takes as much pride in his association with his teammates Merlin Olsen, Rosey Grier, and Lamar Lundy who together formed the Rams' "Fearsome Foursome."

"If you want to get technical about it, the Vikings' 'Purple People Eaters,' the Steelers' 'Steel Curtain' and the Cowboys' 'Doomsday Defense' all came after the Fearsome Foursome," Jones said. "Those teams saw how devastating a great defensive line could be and they wanted to be like us. They had their own nicknames but none of those names were as good as ours and I truly believe that we were the best defensive line to play—in our era or any other."

While Olsen was a great player and a Hall of Famer in his own right, it was Jones who gave the Rams' defensive line its tremendous ability to turn a game around in an instant. "Deacon Jones was not just the best defensive lineman to play the game," Olsen said. "He was the best defensive player ever and from my perspective he was the best all-around football player I ever saw."

George Allen, who cut his teeth as a coach under George Halas, could not give enough credit to Jones for his all-around defensive ability. "No one has ever had his combination of speed, instinct, intelligence, motivation, and drive," Allen said.

Jones never had any doubts about his own all-around ability. "I had a lot of confidence," Jones said. "To be a great football player, you have to have confidence. It helps to be a little angry, too. I also was that. Frustration builds inner drive . . . at least it did for me."

That drive resulted in his inventing not only the term that has become such a big part of today's game but his devastating head slap as well. If he wanted to go inside the tackle, Jones would come with his outside arm and then follow with a blow from his inside one. If he wanted to go outside, it was just the opposite.

"Many defensive ends had their own version of the head slap," Jones explained. "They would take their arm, deliver the shot and off they would go. I could hit the offensive tackle twice before somebody else could do it once. That's what made it so effective."

Jones, always with the twinkle in his eye, knows that he is anything but modest. He doesn't really care because he knows he's telling it the way it was when he dominated for the Rams.

#9

REGGIE WHITE

His outsized personality preceded him wherever he went. There is no doubt that Reggie White was a beloved figure in a game that demands violence. His teammates loved him, his coaches loved him and even some of the quarterbacks he devastated loved him.

That love and his off-the-field life as a minister almost obscure how great a player Reggie White was for the Philadelphia Eagles and the Green Bay Packers. He lifted both of those franchises on his considerable shoulders and helped them regain the credibility that had been missing for so many years.

White's greatest fame as a player probably came in a Green Bay uniform as he helped the Packers win Super Bowl XXXI by registering three sacks in the Packers' 35–21 win over the New England Patriots. However, he was probably a better player when he played for the Eagles from 1985 through 1992. White was such a dynamic combination of muscle and strength that he simply could not be stopped. His first year in the NFL came on the heels of a spring season in the ill-fated United States Football League with the Memphis Showboats. White had 11.5 sacks while playing in Memphis that year and then took a deep breath and put on his Eagles uniform. He had another 13 sacks while playing for the Eagles and quickly established himself as the best defensive end in the league.

White credited much of his NFL success to what he learned in the USFL under defensive-line coach Chuck Dickerson. White was a speed-and-power player as an All-American at the University of Tennessee, with dominant talent. Dickerson refined that talent and taught White many of the moves he used for years. "Chuck showed me how to add finesse to my power and speed," White wrote in his book, *In the Trenches*. "In many ways, my USFL years were the most enjoyable of my career."

The moves White was talking about, such as the spin move, the rip, and the club became staples of White's game and were nearly impossible for opposing offensive linemen to contend with. Despite his background as a minister and his love for his fellow man, he had no problem reconciling the violent game he dominated throughout his career. He led the NFL in sacks with 21 in 1987 and followed that with a league-leading 18 in 1988.

While picking up an offseason award in Chicago after the Packers' win over the Patriots, I was able to sit down with Reggie and talk to him about his ability to overwhelm opponents with his speed and strength. "I love the game and I love that God gave me the ability to do what I do and dominate my opponents," White said. "This game is not in conflict with what I believe. It is just part of the testing process. I am trying to overpower the man on the other side of the line. I know he is trying to do the same to me. At no point when I'm playing do I ever not love my opponent. That's the test I face. Can I still love someone who I am trying to punish? Yes I can."

While White was dominating for the Eagles and Packers, Bruce Smith was doing the same thing for the Buffalo Bills. They were the two best defensive ends of their era but White was viewed as the more complete player because of his dominance against the run and his superior strength. Smith may have been as quick or maybe even a tad quicker than White and had more moves, but he was not the physical player that White was.

ESPN analyst Mark Schlereth was an excellent offensive lineman who won three Super Bowls with the Washington Redskins and Denver Broncos and he knew that facing White was an all-but-impossible task to handle. "Reggie White was one of the greatest football players I've ever seen or lined up against," Schlereth said. "He was amazingly dominant and someone that a team spent a week preparing for. When an offensive line stepped onto the field, it was imperative to locate where White was lined up to have some semblance of a chance at figuring out how he was going to disrupt your offense.

"I'll never forget one of the first times I ever had to face White on the field," Schlereth continued. "I was playing for the Washington Redskins at the time, and I didn't really expect to have to face him. At the time, the Eagles would switch him all over the line so that he'd occasionally face a guard. I'll never forget how I felt when I came out of the huddle and realized he was lining up to face me. I immediately started wondering what I'd done to deserve this butt whupping."

White would go on to become one of the most pivotal figures in Green Bay Packers history. The Packers had become an ordinary team in the quarter-century that had passed since Vince Lombardi had coached them. They had only six winning seasons during that time frame and had been to the playoffs just twice. More than that, Green Bay had developed a reputation as a city that had little to offer to African-American players, and there were a number of complaints about the limited opportunities to make outside money, socialize, and enjoy their existence.

But when free agency came to the NFL after the 1992 season, White signed a four-year, $17 million deal with the Packers and shocked the league with his choice. White's status as one of the leaders of the game helped the Packers bring in other African-American stars such as Sean Jones, Andre Rison, and Keith Jackson and turn the franchise around . . . with the help of quarterback Brett Favre.

White finished his career with 198 sacks, second only to Smith's 200. His untimely death in 2004 at age 43 from sarcoidosis was as shocking as it was untimely. The joyous White had dominated his game and was arguably the best defensive end of his, or any, era.

Reggie White

REGGIE WHITE TEAM DEFENSIVE RANKINGS			
Year	Team	Def. rank	Sacks by White
1985	PHI	10	13
1986	PHI	12	18
1987	PHI	25	21
1988	PHI	14	18
1989	PHI	5	11
1990	PHI	12	14
1991	PHI	5	15
1992	PHI	6	14
1993	GB	9	13
1994	GB	5	8
1995	GB	4	12
1996	GB	1	8.5
1997	GB	5	11
1998	GB	11	16
2000	CAR	12	5.5
TOTAL			198

#10

TOM BRADY

He was just another guy who wanted to play pro football.

When Tom Brady left the University of Michigan following the 1999 season, there was a pretty good chance he would get drafted.

But he was definitely not a star. He might get taken in the fifth, sixth, or seventh round, and he would have a chance to win a spot as a backup quarterback. When it came to things like starting, winning, and collecting championships, that did not appear to be in Brady's grasp.

But the New England Patriots decided to take a chance on Brady in the 2000 NFL Draft. Head coach Bill Belichick thought Brady was worthy of a sixth-round pick, and he made him the 199th player selected that year. Brady was going to get the chance to back up Drew Bledsoe, and that meant holding a clipboard on the sidelines and learning the plays.

That's what Brady did in his rookie year, and he threw just three passes that season. However, when Bledsoe suffered a sheared blood vessel in his chest after getting hammered against the New York Jets, the Patriots turned over their offense and their team to Brady.

It has turned out be one of the most fortuitous moves in the history of the franchise. It shouldn't have been, because Brady was still the same skinny, unathletic quarterback he had been when the Patriots drafted him.

However, he knew the playbook backwards and forwards and he was blessed with the confidence that he could exploit any opponent.

Brady would go on to become one of the best quarterbacks in the history of the game, and he would lead New England to three Super Bowl championships and five appearances in the big game.

Instead of being intimidated by his circumstances, Brady was invigorated by them.

While he did not have the greatest arm strength or the quickest release, Brady quickly showed he was able to diagnose exactly what the defense wanted to do and make the right play call at the key moment.

Brady also possessed unfailing accuracy with his passes. Since New England was a team with a strong defense and a productive ground game in 2001, he did not have to throw the ball all over the lot to win games.

He simply had to take what the defense gave him and deliver the ball to his receivers in a place where they could catch it and still protect themselves at the right time.

Brady exceeded all of Belichick's expectations during that season. After taking over for Bledsoe, he led the Patriots to an 11-3 record.

He completed 264 of 413 passes for 2,843 yards with 18 touchdowns and 12 interceptions.

More than the numbers, it was Brady's manner that converted the New England lockerroom and the coach's room into believers. He played with a confidence that no sixth-round draft choice had the right to possess. He played as if he knew he would always make the right choice and come through at the biggest moment.

If that violated NFL protocol, Belichick was not about to tell him. He certainly wasn't going to say anything when the Pats met the heavily favored St. Louis Rams in Super Bowl XXXVI in New Orleans.

The Pats were upstarts who had managed to overcome the Oakland Raiders and Pittsburgh Steelers to earn their spot in the Super Bowl. The Rams were an offensive juggernaut with Kurt Warner at quarterback and all-purpose stud Marshall Faulk at the running back position.

Brady played with the same poise and guile that he had demonstrated throughout the season. He completed 16-of-27 passes for 145 yards with one touchdown and he did not throw an interception. His scoring pass to David Patten near the end of the second quarter gave the Patriots a 14-3 halftime lead.

But the Rams would mount a second-half comeback that would see them tie the score at 17-17 with 1:30 remaining. Overtime was seemingly on the horizon, as Belichick was not about to trust Brady in the final stages of the fourth quarter.

Well, that's what most of the football world believed, but it was not true. Belichick turned Brady loose and the second-year quarterback directed an eight-play, 53-yard drive that set up placekicker Adam Vinatieri with a game-winning 48-yard field goal attempt.

Vinatieri blasted the ball through the uprights, the Patriots won the Super Bowl, and the legend of Brady was born.

He would go on to lead the Patriots to two more Super Bowl titles in the next three seasons, and that initial championship was the trigger that led Brady to the top of the football world.

He has had a Hall of Fame career that has seen him complete 4,178 passes in 6,586 attempts while throwing for 49,149 yards with 359 touchdowns and 134 interceptions through the 2013 NFL season.

While the numbers have allowed Brady to take a spot with the top quarterbacks in the history of the game, the yardage and touchdown totals have never been his driving factors.

"It's great to put up yardage totals and throw for a lot of touch-downs, but it's only great when it helps your team win," Brady explained in 2012. "That's the reason for playing football, and that has always driven me no matter what level I have played at. We are out there to win games and championships and every player has to do what they are capable of to help their team win.

"If that means throwing short passes, medium-range passes, or long passes, that's just what I will do. If it means handing the ball off 15 times in a row, that's what I am going to do. That's why I have played and that's why I continue to play. Simply to win. I want another championship and another ring."

Few have done it better than Brady over the years.

He may not have had the strongest arm, the most picture-perfect delivery, or been as athletic as the top quarterbacks in the game, but it's hard to find anyone who has been a better leader or more productive throughout his brilliant career.

TOP POSTSEASON WINNERS AMONG QUARTERBACKS (POST-MERGER)

Quarterback	Team	W	L	Pct.
1. Tom Brady	NE	18	8	0.692
2. Joe Montana	SF-KC	16	7	0.696
3. Terry Bradshaw	Pitt	14	5	0.737
4. John Elway	Den	14	8	0.636
5. Brett Favre	GB-Minn.	13	11	0.542
6. Troy Aikman	Dal	11	5	0.688
7. Roger Staubach	Dal	12	6	0.667
8. Peyton Manning	Ind.-Den.	11	12	0.478
9. Ben Roethlisberger	Pitt.	10	4	0.714
10. Kurt Warner	St. L-Ariz.	9	4	0.692

PEYTON MANNING VS. TOM BRADY (THROUGH 2013 SEASON)

Tom Brady

G	GS	QBrec	Cmp	Att	Cmp%	Yds	TD	Int	Y/A	Y/C	Y/G	Rate
193	191	148-43-0	4178	6586	63.4	49149	359	134	7.5	11.8	254.7	95.7

Peyton Manning

G	GS	QB Rec	Comp	Att	Comp %	Yds	TD	Int	Y/A	Y/C	Y/G	Rtg
240	240	167-73-0	5532	8432	65.5	64964	491	219	7.7	11.7	270.7	97.2

#11

DICK BUTKUS

It had the look of a grudge match. When Dick Butkus was drafted by George Halas in the first round of the 1965 draft—the same round that he also selected Gale Sayers—the Chicago Bears already had a Hall of Fame middle linebacker on their roster by the name of Bill George. While George was nearing the end of his career, he truly was an old bear who was being backed into the corner by the young phenom from the University of Illinois.

Most expected George to put on a fearsome display in order to impress Halas and show the rookie he was not about to go easily. For his part, Butkus thought he had hurt his own chances of winning the Bears' starting middle linebacker job by practicing with the college

All-Stars as they prepared to play the defending NFL champion Cleveland Browns in an exhibition prior to the start of the season. But from the minute Butkus came into camp, his intensity set him apart and he thoroughly impressed George.

"He came into camp and started playing hard and dominating," George recalled. "It took me about two practices to realize that I was going to be packing my gear. There was no way that Dick Butkus was not going to be great. He was too fast, too smart, too athletic, and too mean. Nobody could block him. Nobody could slow him down."

In a game dominated by the most violent of athletes, Butkus brought the violence to a new level and perhaps one that has never been surpassed. Butkus was an intimidator who would just as soon send a running back to the hospital as tackle him. A healthy Dick Butkus wanted to impose his will on everyone on the field. That included his own teammates.

Perhaps no Bears player knew what made Dick Butkus tick more than his longtime teammate Doug Buffone. An outstanding player in his own right, Buffone played outside linebacker while Butkus was manning the middle for the Bears. "Dick was not always an easy guy to play with," Buffone explained. "He wanted things done his way, but more than that he wanted to succeed. If the offense had a play that gained yards, got a first down, or God forbid resulted in a touchdown, Dick wanted answers. He wanted to know how we could allow something like that to happen. He knew he hadn't done anything wrong and he wanted to know who was responsible. We always knew he was right. He was a guy who was not about to let any opportunity slip through his grasp and he was not going to be the player who let us down."

Butkus played in an era before stats on tackles were kept with any regularity. However, according to unofficial counts kept by the Bears, Butkus averaged 120 tackles and 58 assists over the first eight years of his career. He also had a career-high 18 sacks during the 1967 season, a shockingly high total for a middle linebacker.

More than tackles, Butkus used his strength and athletic ability to take the ball away from his opponents. He forced 47 turnovers during his nine-year career, including 22 interceptions. He could mug you and take your lunch money but he could also dance once he made an interception. The NFL did not keep stats on forced fumbles during Butkus's tenure but if they had, he would have led the league most seasons he was healthy.

Butkus was a first-team All-Pro in seven of his nine seasons. Playing at the same time as Ray Nitschke of the Green Bay Packers, Lee Roy Jordan of the Dallas Cowboys, and Tommy Nobis of the Atlanta Falcons only underscores how dominant Butkus was. All were great players and Nitschke may have been almost as nasty as Butkus, but none could cover the ground that Butkus could when he had a full head of steam.

As tough as he was, Butkus played the game without developing a reputation for dirty play. He may have stormed, stomped, spit, and intimidated, but he did not eye gouge, kick, or otherwise try to maim players when he tackled. "That was not the way I was going to play," Butkus said. "If you were scared I was going to hurt you, that's one thing. But I was not going to try to do something to a player that went outside the rules."

Butkus's mean streak on the field was something he worked carefully to bring out in his personality and then project to his opponents. "I would always find something to get mad at on game day," Butkus said. "It helped me play my best game. I would look at the other side and maybe I just despised the uniform I was looking at. Or I would see someone on the other team laughing or joking. I would think they were laughing at me or the Bears. That made me angry."

In a game in which players want to prove who is toughest and meanest, Butkus was the hands-down winner nearly every time he took the field. MacArthur Lane was a solid running back for the St. Louis Cardinals when Butkus played for the Bears and he remembers seeing an individual who seemed to be built differently than any other player.

"All I ever thought about when I was on the field at the same time as Butkus was being able to get up after he hit me," Lane said. "That's how tough he was and that's the kind of player he was. He hit harder than any man I was ever tackled by."

Butkus's brilliant career ended after knee and leg injuries prevented him from playing without excruciating pain. Butkus had dealt with the pain throughout his career, but by the 1973 season he could no longer run more than a few steps without searing pain running up and down his leg. He eventually received a settlement from the Bears for the way his leg injury was handled by the team's doctors. But the slow and limping Butkus at the end of his career bore no resemblance to the angry Bear that had dominated the Chicago defense for nearly a decade.

#12

BARRY SANDERS

It's not going out on a limb to say that Barry Sanders was the most elusive running back in the NFL in the post–World War II era. Sanders may have been the most elusive player ever, but there's no need to compare him to Red Grange, who was essentially the make-or-break player in the NFL when he was taken by George Halas on a barnstorming tour across the country back in the 1920s. However, after that tour was over, Grange played much of his career with an injured knee.

Sanders was a throwback in many ways because he was all about playing the game and running the football and had no interest in self-promotion, endorsements, or publicity. What he did have an interest in was making would-be tacklers miss. He was as good as any back who has ever played at making explosive plays and his 10-year career with the Detroit Lions was a monument to his quickness, explosiveness, and ability to confound opposing defenses.

Sanders served notice when he won the Heisman Trophy at Oklahoma State, but the NFL is strewn with Heisman failures. Sanders came in charging, fully confident in his ability to embarrass defenders with his talent for changing direction on a dime. Sanders could literally jump out of the way when faced with an oncoming tackler. No player had his lateral agility and that's one of the reasons he was able to make so many great defensive players look so foolish. Vince Tobin was the defensive coordinator of the Chicago Bears when Sanders came into the league and remained in that position through the 1992 season. He saw Sanders twice a year in his first four seasons, and even though he was considered one of the best defensive game-planners of his era, he knew there was not much he could do against Sanders.

"You could come up with the best game plan in the world against Barry and you could make it work for three quarters of the game and he would be completely hemmed in," Tobin said. "But then he would make something happen because of his leg strength and ability to get out of trouble. He had the ability to jump sideways and create a lane for himself. Nobody else could do that so how could you prepare for it? He's hemmed in and you are just about to crush him and he jumps sideways and he's gone. Nobody else could do that and I don't think anyone else will."

Sanders didn't just frustrate coaches. He turned Hall of Fame players into unabashed fans who couldn't believe their eyes. Fellow Heisman winner Marcus Allen was a brilliant back with the Raiders and Chiefs and will forever be remembered for his 74-yard touchdown run for the silver and black in Super Bowl XVIII against the Washington Redskins.

"I'd be watching the highlights on Sunday night and they would come to the Lions and Barry," Allen recalled. "They'd show one of his runs and I'd be standing there with my mouth open. Then they'd show another and I couldn't just sit there. I had to get on the phone. I might call Eric Dickerson or some other back. I'd say, 'Yo, Dickerson, did you see what he did this time?' That's how good he was. I never even thought of doing that with anybody else."

The late Walter Payton never lacked for self-confidence, but when he saw Sanders run with the ball, his opinion was definitive. "He was the best I ever saw," Payton said. "He was better than me. I could not do the things he could do."

Sanders ranks third all-time in NFL rushing yards, trailing only Emmitt Smith and Walter Payton. He had amassed 15,269 yards when he unexpectedly retired before the 1999 season. He decided that breaking Payton's record of 16,726 yards was not all that important to him and it was Smith, who started in the NFL a year after Sanders, who eventually surpassed Payton's mark.

Sanders had 14 games of at least 100 yards rushing in 1997 alone, the most ever in a single NFL season. He had 76 100-yard games in his career, second only to Payton's 77. He scored 109 career touchdowns (99 rushing) and rushed for at least 1,100 yards in every season he played.

San Francisco 49ers head coach Mike Singletary made the Hall of Fame as a middle linebacker with the Bears. He played against Sanders eight times from 1989 through 1992 and that was enough to convince Singletary that Sanders was among the all-time greats.

"We had a pretty good defense with the Bears and we really didn't pay much attention when we heard there was this back in Detroit who was pretty elusive," Singletary said. "We were not going to be worried about some college star. But then when the first game started it was obvious that we hadn't prepared adequately. He was too quick and too explosive. After that first game, we never took him lightly again but it really didn't matter. He understood what it took to make big plays and he hit us lots of times.

"Part of the problem was his size. There were times when we just couldn't find him behind the line of scrimmage. He was 5-foot-8 and he knew how to make himself look even smaller. So if you needed a split second to find him, there was no way you were ever going to be able to catch him."

Frustrated by the lack of progress that the Lions had made and realizing that he had put in 10 outstanding years, Sanders walked away from the game and never came back. Detroit fans wanted nothing more than to see Sanders put on his No. 20 uniform and play again, but Sanders felt he had done enough.

"Why did I retire" Sanders asked. "My desire to not play was greater than my desire to play. It was just that simple."

Sanders left $20.9 million in salary on the table when he walked away. "Maybe it wasn't the best business decision but it was the right decision for me and I've never regretted it for a minute."

CONSECUTIVE 1,000-YARD RUSHING SEASONS	
Player	**Seasons**
1. Emmitt Smith, Dallas (1991–2001)	11
2. Barry Sanders, Detroit (1989–1998)	10
3. Curtis Martin, New England/New York Jets (1995–2005)	9
4. LaDainian Tomlinson, San Diego (2001–2008)	8
Thurman Thomas, Buffalo (1989–1996)	8
6. Eric Dickerson, Los Angeles Rams/Indianapolis (1983–1989)	7

CONSECUTIVE 1,000-YARD SEASONS TO BEGIN CAREER	
Player	**Seasons**
1. Barry Sanders, Detroit (1989–1998)	10
2. Curtis Martin, New England/New York Jets (1995–2005)	9
3. LaDainian Tomlinson, San Diego (2001–2008)	8
4. Eric Dickerson, Los Angeles Rams/Indianapolis (1983–1989)	7

Barry Sanders

CAREER 1,500-YARD RUSHING SEASONS

Player	Seasons
1. Barry Sanders, Detroit (1991, 1994–1997)	5
2. Eric Dickerson, Los Angeles Rams/Indianapolis (1983–1984, 1986, 1988)	4
Walter Payton, Chicago (1977, 1979, 1984–1985)	4

CONSECUTIVE 1,500-YARD RUSHING SEASONS

Player	Seasons
Barry Sanders, Detroit (1994–1997)	4
Tiki Barber, New York Giants (2004–2006)	3
Terrell Davis, Denver (1996–1998)	3
Earl Campbell, Houston Oilers (1979–1980)	2
Eric Dickerson, Los Angeles Rams (1983–1984)	2
Priest Holmes, Kansas City (2001–2002)	2
Edgerrin James, Indianapolis (1999–2000)	2
Walter Payton, Chicago (1984–1985)	2
O. J. Simpson, Buffalo (1975–1976)	2
Emmitt Smith, Dallas (1991–1992)	2
LaDainian Tomlinson, San Diego (2002–2003)	2

#13

BOB LILLY

The record shows the Dallas Cowboys started to become "America's Team" sometime during the 1966 season. That's the year they won the NFL's Eastern Conference with a 10-3-1 record and earned a spot in the NFL Championship Game against the Green Bay Packers. Green Bay came down to Dallas and bested the Cowboys, 34–27, in a game that came down to a Packers interception of Don Meredith in their own end zone.

The Cowboys had some names on offense in those days—Meredith, Bob Hayes, and Dan Reeves to name a few—but Dallas was able to rise from rank expansion team to championship contender because of the strength of the defense. The architect of that defense was head coach Tom Landry and the star of that unit was defensive tackle Bob Lilly.

The NFL was largely a running league in the 1960s and Landry had come up with a defense that was designed to stop the run. Landry's Flex defense took two of the defensive linemen off the line of scrimmage and dropped them back a step or two in order to give them a better pursuit angle on running backs. Nobody took advantage of that angle or that extra space more than Bob Lilly.

To say the Flex was Landry's baby is accurate, but he got input into the defense from Vince Lombardi when both men were with the New York Giants in the 1950s. Landry was a defensive back and later an assistant coach with New York while Lombardi was also an assistant coach under Jim Lee Howell. The two talked often. Lombardi offered insight as to what defensive formations he thought caused problems and Landry told him which offensive schemes caused the defense problems. Interestingly, the emotional Lombardi would get quite upset if his offensive team got handled by the Giants defense in practice.

Landry knew the Flex was a solid formation but he needed the right players to make it work. The key came when the Cowboys drafted Lilly in the first round of the 1961 draft out of Texas Christian University. With size, strength, and incredible quickness, Lilly appeared to be a very special defensive end who could give the Cowboys the defensive push they needed.

Lilly played defensive end in his first three seasons but prior to the start of the 1964 season, Landry realized the Flex defense would get the boost it needed if Lilly moved inside to tackle. "Bob had all the characteristics you want in a defensive lineman," Landry recalled during an interview prior to Super Bowl XXXII between the Denver Broncos and Green Bay Packers in January of 1998. "He was fast, smart, strong, and quick and while he had been drafted as a defensive end, we came to the conclusion that he could be a real difference maker at tackle. It would put him closer to the action and the Flex would allow him to take better angles to the ball.

"And as much as we thought it would work before we made the move, it worked out even better. Bob was so smart and intuitive that he had that extra edge and could ruin most plays. It was a good defense but what made it work so well was having great players and I don't know how you can get better than Bob Lilly."

Landry, of course, was a stoic leader during his long tenure on the sidelines and was hesitant to pass out the compliments. But Lilly always knew he was doing his job and that he was getting approval from perhaps the most demanding coach of his time.

Lilly was an 11-time Pro Bowl selection and a seven-time All-NFL first-team selection. He was the first Cowboy player to be placed in the Texas Stadium Ring of Honor and was a 1980 inductee in the Hall of Fame, his first year of eligibility. He had 94.5 unofficial sacks in his career (sacks were not counted officially until 1982) and made one of the most famous plays in Super Bowl history when he sacked Miami Dolphins quarterback Bob Griese for a 29-yard loss in Super Bowl VI.

That game, a 24–3 Cowboy victory, was the proudest moment of Lilly's Cowboys career. "You'll remember that we had lost the Super Bowl the year before [16–13 to the Baltimore Colts] and it was such a painful memory," Lilly said. "Everyone had said the Cowboys couldn't win the big one. But when we beat Miami, it showed we were a great team and we could win that big one. We got that monkey off of our back."

Lilly, Joe Greene of the Pittsburgh Steelers, and Merlin Olsen of the Los Angeles Rams were all comparable players. Greene had similar quickness and speed to Lilly while Olsen was nearly as prepared and strong as Lilly. However, neither player could match Lilly when it came to consistency since he played in 196 consecutive games.

Modern defensive tackles like Warren Sapp and John Randle got their job done with penetration and intensity, but neither could match Lilly in strength.

Bob Lilly

"A man like Lilly comes along once in a lifetime," Landry said in 1972. "He is something a little bit more than great. Nobody is better than Bob Lilly."

As great as the Cowboys' 'Doomsday Defense' was in the late 1960s and early 1970s, Lilly believes that the unit's time has come and gone and that it would have very little chance of succeeding against modern-day NFL competition. "More than anything else, the Flex defense was about stopping the run," Lilly said. "Coach Landry came up with it at a time when teams were trying to run the ball at least 60 percent of the time. If they hadn't been trying to run the ball that much, it wouldn't have worked. Teams don't do that anymore. The game changed in the late 1970s and the 1980s and it's now completely different. Teams that try to run the ball as their primary form of offense can't do it. You have to mix in the run and get some kind of balance but you have to be able to throw it. The Flex was all about getting the best angles to stop the run. That wouldn't matter so much anymore."

But it mattered then and Lilly dominated against the run like few others have been able to do.

#14

RONNIE LOTT

San Francisco's ascension to NFL dominance is largely credited to head coach Bill Walsh and quarterback Joe Montana. The 49ers became an offensive juggernaut and Walsh's "West Coast Offense" became the team's legacy. Montana, and later Steve Young, served as the triggerman and receivers Dwight Clark, Freddie Solomon, Jerry Rice, and John Taylor lit up the scoreboard along with running backs Roger Craig, Wendell Tyler, and Ricky Watters.

Walsh and Montana were the two most visible parts of the team but neither one claimed to be the most important. Both would refrain from answering questions regarding who the best or most important player on the team was but if they were pushed to the wall, each man gave the same answer: Ronnie Lott.

Ronnie Lott

Lott started his NFL career as a cornerback with the Niners but he was quickly used at both safety positions in addition to his coverage duties at cornerback. As a rookie, he immediately imposed his will on his defensive teammates. The 49ers had simply been a soft defensive team before Lott arrived on the scene. They were drag-down tacklers and allowed points by the bushel. The 1980 Niners finished 6–10 and surrendered 415 points.

Lott knew he was coming to a team that almost never came up with the key stops and rarely contributed a big hit. He knew why they had drafted him and he was bound and determined to turn things around.

"Teams had basically done whatever the Dallas wanted to the 49ers," Lott said. "There had been a game against the Cowboys that year where they had just gotten destroyed, 59–14, and they had just pushed the Niners around from start to finish. There had been no resistance. That game cut a hole in the team's psyche and I knew that it would never go away until we could stand up to them.

"That's one of the things I felt I had to do. Give the team something to fight for. Put a chip on its shoulder. We had to have some toughness. I was more than happy to do whatever I could. If that meant flying around like a missile, I would do just that."

Walsh had seen the characteristics of leadership and dominance when he watched Lott on tape as he prepared for the 1981 draft. That toughness was even more apparent when he talked to Lott one-on-one.

"We were starting to get better from an offensive perspective but we didn't have the presence to be a good team because the defense was so far behind," Walsh said. "There was no question that we needed to be a lot tougher and Ronnie Lott was going to give us that. I thought he might be the right guy just from looking at his films, but when I talked to him it became crystal clear. We needed him to be on the field if we were going to get better."

Montana felt the same way as his coach. He thought the offense had a chance to come around but there was nothing on the defensive side that gave him any comfort. "You play to win and we felt that we were going to improve offensively," Montana said of the team preparing for the 1981 season. "But the defense had been awful and nobody thought we were going to get any better [on that side of the ball]. But that summer we saw Ronnie hitting everything in sight. It was clear things were going to get better because he was on the field."

The X-factor for Lott was his leadership. How many rookies can provide it? Rookies who tend to talk and say what's on their mind generally get slapped down and called a punk. But Lott had the gift for speaking the truth without stepping on his elders' toes. He became a very vocal leader in the years that followed but even as a rookie he was able to say important things to older teammates.

"I guess they thought I was sincere," Lott said. "Maybe [it was] because of the way I played. They could see I left it all on the field every day so I could speak my mind."

Lott was a devastating hitter, but he also had the hands to intercept the ball. He had 63 interceptions in his career, good for sixth all-time, and led the league in interceptions in both 1986 and 1991. Five of his interceptions he returned for touchdowns. He also delivered 1,113 punishing tackles—plus 8.5 sacks—during his 14-year career, earning 10 Pro Bowl selections and six selections to the All-Pro team. He caused 16 fumbles and he recovered 17 more. If there was someone to be hit, Lott was more than willing to lay the lumber.

As productive as Lott was, he wished he had been better when the ball was in the air. "I had a few interceptions but I never could catch the ball the way I wanted to," Lott said. "If there was one thing I could change about my game, that would be it. I see a guy like Ed Reed and the way he goes after the ball and I think that's how I would like to have played. He's magical going after the ball. I wasn't anything close to that."

Perhaps Lott is being a bit hard on himself or perhaps he's right. But if he had poor hands he had a pretty good excuse. Half of his left pinky finger had been removed in 1985 after it got caught up in an opponent's facemask and had been mangled. Lott wasn't interested in an operation or rehab—he wanted to go back on the field. Lott instructed the surgeon to "cut it off."

"That story is so old," Lott said. "You don't have to tell it again. I think people know what happened."

Yes they do. But it gives an indication of what the Niner veterans learned about Lott during his rookie year. "I wanted to play and I wanted to win. It was just that simple. Who knows when I would have been back if I had surgery. I wanted to get back onto the field. That's where it all happened."

Lott's impact is underrated because the 49ers were such a big-time offensive team with Joe Montana, Roger Craig, Dwight Clark, and Jerry Rice gathering so many of the headlines. But Lott's defensive impact was not underrated in the San Francisco locker room. "As offensive players, we had our own business to attend to when we were on the sidelines," Montana said. "But after we talked about what we would do next, you had your eye on the defense. You wanted to see who Ronnie was going to hit next."

#15

ANTHONY MUNOZ

There was nothing brutish about the way Anthony Munoz played football. He was a big man for his time and exceptionally strong and powerful, but Munoz was the top blocker of his time because of his skills and talent. However, don't think for a second that Munoz was not about blasting his opponents into submission. He did it regularly when he finished his blocks.

But even when Munoz was run blocking he would start off with the sweetest technique that NFL observers had ever seen. Munoz learned the finer points of blocking under coach John Robinson at USC and continued to develop once he was drafted third overall by the Cincinnati Bengals in 1980. "I enjoyed what I was doing and I never really thought it was about me showing the other guy who was tougher," Munoz said "I wanted to create a hole for the running back or protect the quarterback. To me, that was all about technique. My technique against his technique. You want to turn it into some physical battle or some war, fine. But that's not going to change my objective. I want to open a hole. I want to create a running lane. I want to protect the quarterback. I'm not going to get drawn into your war."

When Munoz was playing left tackle for the Bengals, he opened huge holes in the running game. Eleven times chosen to the Pro Bowl and a nine-time first-team All-Pro selection, Munoz led Cincinnati to the most productive running game in the league from 1986 to 1989, when almost all the key runs were to his side of the ball.

James Brooks was a very good running back, but he is never going to be compared with Barry Sanders, Walter Payton, or Emmitt Smith. Yet when he was running behind Munoz, he was one of the most feared backs in the league. "I didn't feel like I needed that much room to make a big play," Brooks said. "I was quick and I could get through a small crack. But when you run behind Anthony you don't get a small crack. He was so big, so powerful, and just so good that you got a whole lane to run through and then you could cut off his back as he was finishing his block. He was like nobody I ever played with."

Munoz was a student of the game and he was blessed with a tap dancer's feet. He could sprint when he had to in order to make a block on the corner but what made him superior was his ability to change direction without losing his balance.

"I don't care who he was playing against, what the conditions were like or what his assignment was," said longtime Bengals offensive-line coach Jim McNally. "He never fell down. He had the most incredible balance I've ever seen. Even against the quickest pass rushers he would never leave his feet. He had incredible balance and anticipation. He was a great player to coach and just a tremendous student of the game."

Munoz actually viewed himself as something of an artist on the field. He viewed offensive-line play as the most unsung aspect of football and his goal was to play the position to perfection. His wife DeDe offered perhaps the best insight of anyone when it came to Munoz's career. "If you really watch the way he plays offensive line, it's different than any other player in the league," she told *Sports Illustrated*. "Instead of trying to intimidate someone or overpower them, all he wanted to do was show how his skill level was higher than his opponent's. It's artistic the way he plays. He makes it look easy."

Munoz was huge on conditioning but not necessarily the weight-lifting aspect that is such a big part of today's game. Munoz would run two to three miles before practice and then take part in the regular drills that the rest of his team took part in. He pushed himself even harder as he got older. Munoz realized that older players had an edge in knowledge and technique but younger players were more athletic. That's why he kept pushing himself because he never wanted his opponent to have an edge on him.

"I'll tell you that he was one great player," said former Houston Oilers defensive end William Fuller, who would line up against Munoz twice a year. "The man had the most unbelievably quick feet at the position that I ever saw. Nobody was even close. And when you combine that with his technique it was a brutal assignment to try to get the best of him. He had the best feet and his hands were just at about the same level. He was the best and by a wide margin."

Pass blocking was almost easy for Munoz. As he would settle into his backpedal, he got to his blocking position quickly and then would not give another inch. His consistency amazed Ken Anderson and Boomer Esiason, the Bengals' primary quarterbacks when Munoz played each of whom went to a Super Bowl with Munoz up front.

"Here's the thing you have to know about Anthony Munoz," Esiason said. "He always did his job. I don't know anything that's better to say about a professional football player. He didn't use excuses and he didn't need them. He was there to do a job and he did it the way you were supposed to. It didn't matter who he was going up against. Anthony was always there and always holding up his end of the deal. The only thing he didn't do was disappoint you."

In an era when athletes frequently went for the glory and the gusto, there was no element to his game that was about trying to grab credit. "He never said anything when you played against him," said Hall of Fame defensive end Bruce Smith. "No trash talking. No nothing. The only thing I ever heard from him was an apology when his fingers went inside my facemask. If that had happened with other players you would have thought they had done it to get an edge. Not with Anthony. Not only didn't he need to get an edge, he would never have played dirty, not even for a second."

Sounds like the perfect offensive lineman. There aren't too many that would argue the point.

#16

JOE GREENE

Millions of football fans know Joe Greene for his famous Coca-Cola commercial and his infamous nickname. "Mean Joe" was neither the meanest nor the baddest player to ever step on a football field, but he was one of the most dynamic pass rushers and defensive linemen to ever play the game.

Greene wore No. 75 for the Pittsburgh Steelers, perhaps the most famous license plate on the Steel Curtain defense. In a commercial that debuted in Super Bowl XIV in 1980, an exhausted Greene is approached by a 10-year-old boy who offers him a bottle of Coca-Cola and Greene accepts it. After Greene takes a long, satisfying swig of the drink, the boy starts to walk away.

Then, in a booming voice, Greene says, "Hey, kid." The boy turns around and Greene throws him his game-worn jersey.

That commercial, still replayed when the best advertisements in Super Bowl history are shown, came near the end of Greene's career. Before that ad, he earned a reputation as the most feared defensive player on the Steel Curtain. That defensive unit, of course, won four Super Bowls in the 1970s, produced four Hall of Famers (Greene, Jack Lambert, Jack Ham, and Mel Blount), and is generally considered to be the greatest of all-time because they were not one-year wonders like the 1985 Chicago Bears or 2000 Baltimore Ravens.

Greene played his college football at North Texas State, one of the few schools that offered Greene a scholarship. The North Texas nickname is the Mean Green, and Greene's nickname was derived from that.

He lived up to that nickname in his early years with the Steelers. He was drafted by the Steelers in 1969 and was very unhappy that he would have to play for a team that had a history of losing. When Pittsburgh went 1–13 in his rookie year, he was angry most of the time and his snarling and nastiness caused rookie head coach Chuck Noll to sit him down and talk to him on several occasions. However, when the Steelers started to show improvement, Greene bought into Noll's program and became an unquestioned team leader.

Greene could be devastating on the field but his ability was derived from his quickness and instincts. He was one of the first defensive tackles to "tilt" or play at an angle instead of lining up with his shoulders directly opposite his opponents. Greene lived in the guard-center gap and his opponents never knew who he was going to attack.

Greene unveiled that strategy during the 1974 season and it came into play as the Steelers went to Oakland to take on the marauding Raiders in the AFC Championship Game. The Raiders were favored since they were playing at home and many considered their offensive line the equal of the Steelers' defensive line. Taking on

Raiders center Jim Otto and left guard Gene Upshaw—both Hall of Famers—Greene dominated the game and the Steelers spanked the Raiders, 23–14. Two weeks later, Greene was at it again in the Super Bowl against the Minnesota Vikings. Greene punished Vikings center Mick Tinglehoff, generally considered to be the top technician of his era at the position and also a Hall of Famer. At 6-foot-2 and 237 pounds Tinglehoff lacked size, but he was quick and had great technique. Greene's performance helped the Steelers come away with a 16–6 win. His remarkable day included an interception, a forced fumble, and a fumble recovery as the Vikings did not score an offensive touchdown.

The Steelers defense peaked during the first two Super Bowl seasons in 1974 and 1975, ultimately beating the Vikings and Dallas Cowboys in Super Bowls IX and X. But their best performance may have come in 1976 when they refused to let their opponents score. They registered five shutouts that season and held nine of their opponents to single digits. They were prohibitive favorites to get to the Super Bowl after reeling off nine straight wins to close the regular season but injuries to starting running backs Franco Harris and Rocky Bleier limited the offense and the Steelers were beaten by the Raiders in the 1976 AFC Championship Game, 24–7.

"That was the defense that stands out to me," said Greene. "Don't get me wrong because I'm not taking anything away from our Super Bowl teams but we just dominated that year. We got off to a terrible start, losing four of our first five games. Then the switch went on. We shut down the run to the point where teams didn't want to try. Then we choked off the pass. Every unit of the defense worked in synch. It couldn't have been any better. When you have five shutouts you are doing your job. And in some of those games, teams were lucky to get two or three first downs."

The Pittsburgh defensive line was where it all started. As great as the linebackers were—led by Jack Lambert—and as dynamic as the secondary was—led by Mel Blount—it was the defensive line that started it all. Greene, Dwight White, Ernie "Fats" Holmes, and L.C. Greenwood were an unstoppable foursome, as good or better than the front fours of the Rams and Vikings that preceded them. Green, with 66 unofficial sacks in his career, was the best and most fearsome of that group.

#17

RAY LEWIS

Descriptions of football players as tough, ferocious, and intimidating don't often carry much weight.

In a game that is built on controlled violence, anger, and brutality, the majority of players, especially those on the defensive side of the ball, seem to have an innate sense of these traits. If players didn't have these characteristics, they would have stopped playing the game long before their high school careers came to an end.

But there are those players who are just a little bit different than the majority when it comes to emotional makeup. There are players who seem to hit harder than others. Former Chicago Bears linebacker Doug Buffone calls it the Neanderthal gene.

Ray Lewis

Ray Lewis is one of those players who was born to be a football player. He has been one of the hardest hitters and most effective tacklers the game has ever seen.

Lewis had many of the tangible characteristics needed to become the dominant figure on one of the best defenses the NFL has seen in the last 50 years. He had quickness and speed for his position, the strength needed to knock over brutish blockers and explosive running backs, and the intelligence to figure out how the offense was going to attack.

However, it was his intangible characteristics of leadership and ruthlessness on the field that allowed him to rise up to the level of the great players whoever competed.

Lewis's story of success on the football field is compelling, but it is also just part of his tale. He had his best year in 2000 when the Ravens put on a defensive show that rivaled the 1985 Chicago Bears. However, his off-the-field activities in the offseason that preceded that year nearly derailed his career.

Lewis went to a party prior to Super Bowl XXXIV in Atlanta, and by the end of the night, Lewis had a murder charge hanging over his head after a brawl left two men dead outside an Atlanta nightclub.

There was never enough evidence to make the murder charge against Lewis stick, and he would eventually plead guilty to misdemeanor obstruction of justice. However, the event has left a stain against Lewis's reputation and has given his detractors the fuel to question his character.

While those questions have never disappeared completely, it was clear that Lewis was not about to do anything else that could put his NFL career in jeopardy. He was a man on a mission throughout the 2000 season, and the Ravens defense carried the team to remarkable heights.

The Ravens did not have a functional offensive team that year. They did not score an offensive touchdown between Week 5 and Week 9. Head coach Brian Billick had earned his reputation as a record-setting offensive coordinator with the Minnesota Vikings, but he simply did not have the kind of weapons to make a difference in Baltimore.

But he had Lewis, who led a ferocious defense. There were several other top-level defenses in the NFL that season, including that of the Oakland Raiders, the Tennessee Titans, and the New York Giants, but none of them played with the relentlessness of the Ravens.

Lewis had 137 tackles, three sacks, two interceptions, and three fumble recoveries in 2000, and he earned NFL defensive player of the year honors as well as his fourth straight trip to the Pro Bowl.

But individual honors had nothing to do with Lewis's motivation that season. Despite his team's problems on offense, the defense was so strong that Lewis knew that his team was capable of winning a Super Bowl.

"That's why I played football throughout my career," Lewis said. "It was all about winning championships. I wanted to be a champion and I played with guys who wanted the same thing. We could taste it that season, and each week we got better. We didn't just want to get into the playoffs, we wanted to win the whole thing. We knew we had the team to do it because of the way we attacked. Who was going to get the best of us?"

The Ravens played like crazed dogs in playoff victories over the Denver Broncos and Tennessee Titans. They were underdogs when they traveled to Oakland to take on the explosive Raiders, but they stopped quarterback Rich Gannon and that offense in its tracks and earned a spot in Super Bowl XXXV against the Giants.

While Lewis had to deal with non-stop questions about his alleged role in the incident from the previous year, Lewis would not allow himself to be distracted. The Baltimore defense was at its best in that game. They simply did not give the Giants any room to breathe, and it was a matter of choking off the running game, shutting down the passing game, and not giving the Giants any offensive rhythm. New York had no chance in a 34-7 defeat. The only points the Giants scored came on a kickoff return for a touchdown.

Lewis would not win another Super Bowl until his final season in 2012, when the Ravens outlasted the San Francisco 49ers 34–31.

Baltimore was no longer a defensive juggernaut, and Lewis was basically a one-armed player who had lost more than a step by that point in his career. The 49ers gained 484 yards in a game that they were inches away from winning.

Despite the Ravens' struggles on the defensive side of the ball in that game, Lewis and his teammates came up with one final stop with less than two minutes remaining that allowed Baltimore to win the championship.

While he was no longer dominant physically, Lewis's incredible will and leadership were huge factors in bringing Baltimore another Super Bowl title.

"I don't know, at least in my time in the league, if there's been a defensive player that's had as big an impact," said Green Bay Packers head coach Mike McCarthy. "Ray Lewis is really an incredible example of a leader. Talk about somebody opening up his chest and giving his heart to his football team. That's what Ray Lewis did."

TOP RUN DEFENSES SINCE 1970

Team	Year	Attempts	Yards	YPA	Result
1. Baltimore Ravens	2000	361	970	2.69	Won Super Bowl
2. San Diego Chargers	1998	422	1,140	2.70	5–11
3. Minnesota Vikings	2006	348	985	2.83	6–10
4. Baltimore Ravens	2007	446	1,268	2.84	5–11
5. Philadelphia Eagles	1991	383	1,136	2.97	10–6

TOP MLBs (1990-PRESENT)

Player	Tackles	Sacks	Forced Fumbles	Interceptions
Junior Seau	1,522	56.5	11	18
Ray Lewis	1,562	41.5	19	31
Zach Thomas	1,100	20.5	16	17
Brian Urlacher	1,040	41.5	15	22

#18

BRETT FAVRE

Yes, there was a time when Brett Favre was one of the top quarterbacks in the game, ripping defenses with his quick-strike arm and gunslinger mentality.

Favre would become something of a soap opera at the end of his career, and a messy one at that. He couldn't decide whether to retire or not, and once he made his first decision to leave the game, he quickly reversed his field.

That decision made the final seasons of his career quite tortured. But after leaving Green Bay, playing with the Jets, and then finally the Vikings, Favre's brilliant career achievements are starting to regain their luster.

Favre was a star in Green Bay, but he could have made his legacy elsewhere. The Packers picked up Favre from the Atlanta Falcons prior to the 1992 draft, sending a first-round pick to the Falcons for a player they had picked in the second round a year earlier.

Favre would get a chance to play for the Packers early in the 1992 season when starting quarterback Don Majkowski suffered an ankle injury. Favre had struggled in practice sessions and didn't appear to understand the Green Bay game plan, but that all changed after he hit wide receiver Kittrick Taylor with the game-winning touchdown pass against the Cincinnati Bengals.

Favre then made a remarkable transition to the Green Bay offense, starting every game from Week Four of the 1992 season through the end of the 2007 season. Along the way, he proved to be a lot more than someone who just showed up for work every day. He showed one of the strongest arms the game has ever seen, a true gunslinger's mentality and a record of achievement.

Favre won three MVP awards, two offensive player of the year awards, made 11 Pro Bowls, and was named to three first-team All-Pro teams. Through the 2013 season, Favre stands as the NFL's all-time leader in pass attempts (10,169), pass completions (6,300), passing yards (71,838), touchdown passes (508), and interceptions (336).

Those interceptions have been testimony to Favre's fearlessness and recklessness. Throughout the majority of his career, Favre has always believed he could squeeze a ball in through any opening that he saw, even if that opening was less than 18 inches from 35 yards away.

Favre was traded to the New York Jets prior to the 2008 season after a messy divorce from the Packers. Favre had retired in the 2008 offseason but decided he wanted to come back shortly before the start of training camp. The Packers, tired of this annual dance with Favre, had already committed the job to strong-armed quarterback Aaron Rodgers, and they wanted Favre to stick to his original retirement decision. When he didn't, he was traded to the Jets.

The move to Broadway was anything but a hit. Favre looked ordinary and rarely happy in a Jets uniform. The joie de vie that had been such a huge part of his persona during his best days in Green Bay was missing in New York.

Favre rebounded with a brilliant season in Minnesota in 2009, but he could not sustain his abilities when he returned in 2010. He finally called it a career after a forgettable showing with the Vikings that season.

Favre's amazing confidence allowed him to execute throws that few other quarterbacks would even dream of making. In the 1993 Wild Card playoff game against the Lions, Favre was chased out of the pocket to his left by Lion defensive end Robert Porcher. Instead of running or throwing to his left, Favre was nearly on the left sideline when he stopped, pivoted, and threw a perfect 40-yard touchdown pass to Sterling Sharpe down the *right sideline* for the game-winning touchdown in a 28-24 victory.

Favre never lacked belief in his own ability, but that play convinced him that anything was possible. "You have to believe in yourself or you don't have a chance," Favre said. "I know that was a tough throw, but when I made it I felt like I could get it to Sterling without a problem. I wasn't worried."

Favre's career reached its pinnacle when the Packers beat the Patriots 35-21 in Super Bowl XXXI in New Orleans. Favre hit wide receiver Andre Rison with a 54-yard touchdown pass in the first quarter and the Packers never looked back.

They were big favorites to repeat as champions the following year when they faced the Broncos and John Elway in San Diego, but the Broncos would not be denied, and they beat the Packers 31-24.

Elway would lead his team to one more Super Bowl title in his final season, and his two Super Bowl titles would give him an edge that Favre has not been able to overcome.

#19

JOHN ELWAY

The book on John Elway was not completed until the 1997 season, the penultimate year of Elway's career. The numbers had always been big and Elway's physical talent had never been in doubt. He was a remarkable athlete who probably had more arm strength than any other quarterback except Dan Marino and his ability to make plays on the run and keep plays alive was comparable with Steve Young, who makes an appearance later in this list.

Elway proved to be one of the masters of the fourth-quarter comeback throughout his career, but there was one question that had dogged him since he came into the NFL in 1983 after a stellar career at Stanford University. Could he win the big game?

Throughout his career in the NFL, the Denver Broncos had been contenders in the AFC. They had won the conference title three times, but the Broncos had been overwhelmed by the New York Giants, Washington Redskins, and San Francisco 49ers, respectively, in the Super Bowl, with each loss worse than the one before. Careful analysis of what had happened in Super Bowls XXI, XXII, and XXIV revealed that the Broncos were overpowered on both sides of the line of scrimmage and that was the primary reason they lost contact with their opponents. But it was equally undeniable that Elway played poorly in each of those games.

That was clearly the case in San Francisco's 55–10 rout of the Broncos in Super Bowl XXIV. Early in the game, Elway had open receivers to throw the ball to, but he just could not get the ball to them . . . and his attempts were not even close. He threw bounce passes, he threw the ball over their heads, and he just plain missed. At the same time, Joe Montana was razor sharp and he eviscerated the soft Denver defense with throws to Jerry Rice, John Taylor, and Roger Craig.

The disappointment on Elway's face was unmistakable. All he ever wanted was to get another shot at a championship. His impressive yardage, touchdown, and regular-season-win totals meant little to him.

"I was obsessed with getting back to the Super Bowl," Elway said. "I had been there three times and it had ended badly each time. I wanted to win a championship and so did everyone wearing a Denver uniform. It was important to all of us and it was very important as far as my career is concerned. Rightly or wrongly we are judged by how we do in the last game of the year and it was my desire to get there and finally walk off the field with a smile, feeling good about our performance. I was beginning to think that it might not happen."

John Elway

Getting to the Super Bowl is often out of a quarterback's control. However, the numbers that he puts on the board are under his control. Here are some of the more notable numbers in Elway's career:

- Nine-time Pro Bowl selection and six-time Pro Bowl starter
- One NFL MVP (1987)
- One Super Bowl MVP (XXXIII)
- 12 seasons with 3,000 or more yards passing
- 4,123 passes completed
- 300 TD passes
- 51,475 passing yards
- 32 rushing touchdowns
- 47 game-tying or game-winning drives in the fourth quarter

The last figure was probably the most notable number in Elway's career until he led the Broncos to Super Bowl wins over the Green Bay Packers and Atlanta Falcons in the last two years of his career. His ability to lead the Broncos from behind became his signature in the 1986 AFC Championship Game against the Cleveland Browns. In that game, the Broncos walked into Cleveland's ancient Municipal Stadium amid the howling fans in the "Dawg Pound" and the Bernie Kosar–led Browns. Both teams played superbly but the Browns had a 20–13 lead late in the fourth quarter when the Broncos got the ball back at their own 2-yard line following a botched kickoff return. With the Browns defense pinning its ears back and coming after Elway on almost every snap, he marched Denver down the field and hit wide receiver Mark Jackson with a game-tying touchdown pass in the final seconds to send the game into overtime. The Broncos won it in the extra session on a Rich Karlis field goal.

"The Drive" is where Elway's reputation was first built, but it wasn't cemented until a dozen years later when Denver defeated Green Bay in Super Bowl XXXII by a score of 31–24. In that game, Terrell Davis scored the winning touchdown late in the fourth quarter and Elway stood triumphantly on the sideline when the

Broncos defense stopped Brett Favre on a desperation fourth-down pass. Elway came back on the field for one last snap, taking a knee in what he called "the happiest moment of my career."

Broncos owner Pat Bowlen took the Vince Lombardi trophy and held it aloft after the win, hesitated for a moment and then told the crowd: "This one's for John."

That championship had seemed impossible a few years earlier as the Broncos lost much of their luster in the early 1990s. But when Denver hired offensive mastermind Mike Shanahan as head coach in 1995 and also drafted stud running back Terrell Davis from the University of Georgia, the arrow started pointing up for Elway. The partnership with his new coach was especially satisfying because Shanahan gave Elway the opportunity to open up the offense while providing him with a dominant running game. "It was just a great place to be in," Elway said. "We could run the ball. We had a great ground game and nobody could sit back and just wait for the pass. That allowed us to open things up."

After the Super Bowl win over the Packers Elway would line up for one more season and it would end with another Super Bowl win over the Falcons in Super Bowl XXXIII. "To wait so long to get that first Super Bowl was unbelievable," said Elway. "With every-thing we had been through it was unbelievable to get it. But to get another one was sensational and I can't think of a better way to end my career."

It was the validation that he craved and cemented his status as one of the game's all-time great players.

#20

EARL CAMPBELL

Most running backs don't last very long in the NFL. The wear and tear of hard tackling and blocking seems to wear out running backs faster than players at any other position in the NFL. This even applies to the great backs in the game's history. Jim Brown retired at the peak of his powers because he wanted to pursue a film career. But Earl Campbell, "The Tyler Rose," left the game after eight seasons because his body simply had nothing left to give.

Campbell aficionados will remember that he spent his last two years with the New Orleans Saints. Those two years were basically about muscle memory and running on fumes under his former Houston Oilers head coach Bum Phillips. However, when Campbell was in his heyday during six glorious years with the Oilers, he was a combination wrecking ball, sprinter, and running machine.

Campbell's style was all about hard work and inflicting punishment on those who attempted to tackle him. As a result, he wore out after a shorter stay in the NFL then he had planned. Nevertheless, he ranks with the all-time greats in the game's history. Campbell was so strong and powerful that many NFL historians refer to him as strictly a power back. But while he did not have a lot of make-you-miss moves, Campbell also had fine straight-ahead speed and could outrace the defense once he got to the sidelines.

It's hard not to think of the Monday night game against the Miami Dolphins during his 1978 rookie season when thinking of Campbell's top moments. The Oilers beat an excellent Dolphins team that night, 35–30, as Campbell rushed for 199 yards and four touchdowns. The last of those was an 81-yard run down the far sidelines with Dolphins cornerback Curtis Johnson in pursuit. Johnson chased Campbell the last 30 yards of the run but he could not catch him.

"It was a wide running play," said Phillips, "the pitchout. He started and turned up the field. About five people had an angle on him, and two of them were cornerbacks, and they couldn't catch him. Earl never could get caught once he got out into the open."

Phillips knew that Campbell had carried the Oilers to a big win that night and he also knew that Campbell was one yard short of gaining 200 yards. He asked his star if he wanted to go back in to pick up the yard and have a 200-yard night. Campbell, exhausted and sucking oxygen, thanked Phillips and told him to put backup Ronnie Coleman in the game.

Phillips was known as a coach who supported all of his player publicly, but his backing of Campbell knew no limits.

"He was a great back who dominated games with his talent and his heart," Phillips said. "But there was a lot more to him than that. He was so good that he made the offensive linemen blocking for him appear better than they really were. He was so good that he made the quarterback look better than he was. He was so good that he made his coach look a lot smarter than he really was. You can't ask for more from a player than that."

Campbell led the NFL in rushing yards in each of his first three seasons. As a rookie he made his mark by rushing for 1,450 yards and 13 touchdowns while averaging 4.8 yards per carry. It didn't stop there as Campbell was even better his next two seasons. He ran for 1,697 yards and 19 touchdowns his second year and an incredible 1,934 yards and 13 touchdowns while averaging 5.2 yards per carry in year three. That yardage total was the second-highest in NFL history at the time and was just 69 yards behind O. J. Simpson's single-season record of 2,033 yards, set in 1973 (though in a 14-game schedule). Campbell was nearly unstoppable as he put four 200-yard rushing games on the board and continued to overpower defensive players with his bludgeoning forearms.

A two-time league MVP (1978, 1979), three-time offensive player of the year (1978–1980), and five-time All-Pro selection, Campbell's great strength also led to his premature retirement from the game. He never ran out of bounds when he had the opportunity and he seemed to look for contact even if he could cut to the outside to avoid it.

Campbell's overwhelming style won him the respect of the league's best defensive team, the Pittsburgh Steelers. "I was never afraid to tackle anyone and I basically enjoyed it when I had the chance to stick someone," said Steelers Hall of Fame defensive back Mel Blount. "But it was a different story with Campbell. That was a very dangerous man. He inflicted a lot of punishment and a lot of pain. I did what I could against him but it was always a chore and always difficult. Tackling him was like taking a punch from Joe Frazier."

Campbell was still a pounding runner after the Oilers traded him to the Saints during the 1984 season but he didn't have much cartilage left in his knees and his speed had all but disappeared. He ran for 643 yards and averaged 4.1 yards in his final year and had to hang it up, realizing that there was nothing left in the tank. His career was short and explosive and it's doubtful fans will see its like again.

MOST 200-YARD RUSHING GAMES IN A SEASON

Player	Team	Year	200-yard games
Earl Campbell	HOU	1980	4
O. J. Simpson	BUF	1973	3
Tiki Barber	NYG	2005	3

NOTABLE RUNNING BACKS WITH INJURY-SHORTENED CAREERS

Player	Years	Attempts	Yards	YPC	TD
Earl Campbell	9	2,187	9,407	4.3	81
Gale Sayers	7	991	4,956	5.0	39
Bo Jackson	4	515	2,782	5.4	16
Terrell Davis	7	1,655	7,607	4.6	60

#21

JOHN HANNAH

There was a joy in the way John Hannah played offensive line for the New England Patriots. Not the joy of a man who took his assignment, did it well and felt proud afterward. No, with Hannah it went a bit further. Hannah didn't just want to block you to open a hole or protect his quarterback. He wanted to destroy you physically and break your will.

Hannah was not a mean-looking individual but he was transformed on the football field. He played as the Patriots developed from a heartbreaking disappointment to a near-great team between 1973 and 1985, but throughout his tenure on the field, Hannah was just about the meanest man on the field. He would use his forearms to punish defensive linemen while opening up huge holes for running backs like Sam "Bam" Cunningham and Andy Johnson. Both were nice players and Cunningham bordered on stardom. But neither player would have accomplished much if not for the edgy blocking of Hannah, who earned a reputation as one of the toughest men in the NFL—even though he checked in at 6-foot-3 and 265 pounds, a fairly average-sized for a guard during his era.

A nine-time Pro Bowler and seven-time first-team All-Pro selection, Hannah has been called the greatest offensive lineman alive, an honor that makes Hannah proud but one that he shies away from much of the time. "There have been too many great offensive linemen for anyone to call me that," Hannah says.

But he does not dispute that he got everything he could out of his body and always left it all on the field. His work ethic was instilled in him by his father Herb, an offensive lineman who played 12 games for the New York Giants in 1951, and then it was cemented home when he played his college football at the University of Alabama under the legendary Paul "Bear" Bryant.

Bryant's demanding nature and the trials that he put his players through have been part of the great coach's legacy, but Hannah lived through it. Bryant put his team through rigid workouts to prepare for the season by making them go through countless drills and running long distances on 100-degree days in the Alabama sun. As the players would go through their paces, Bryant had no sympathy. "'You feel like you're going to puke and you feel like you're going to die, but you are going to pass out long before that would happen,'" Hannah recalled his coach saying. "You had no choice but to do what he told you to do. That was the law."

Bryant would also decide close position battles by putting first- and second-team players in a circle and the starter would be the one who emerged from the battle victorious. Hannah never lost one of those battles.

John Hannah

The fourth overall pick in the 1973 NFL draft, Hannah gave the Patriots a presence on their offensive line from day one. He had the raw materials and talent to work with when he was drafted but he credits head coaches Chuck Fairbanks and Raymond Berry from getting the most out of him. "Chuck was so organized and he taught me that you can make plans but they only get established when you surround yourself with talent and you consult with wise counsel," Hannah said. "Once you do that, your plans are written in stone."

Hannah's everyday teachers in the NFL were offensive line coaches Red Miller and Jim Ringo. "Red helped me to appreciate everything I had and give the most I could on every snap," Hannah said. "What greater pleasure can you have in life than to do the thing you like doing the most. For me, that meant playing pro football. I appreciated it every minute.

"With Jim, it was all about taking the level you were at and then getting better. He got his point across that once you establish what your base is, you have to get better and better or else you are slipping back. I understood that and I agreed with it."

While Hannah credits his coaches for getting the most out of him, Fairbanks, Berry, Miller, and Ringo all described Hannah as the most focused offensive lineman that they ever saw. If ever there was a player who didn't need outside motivation it was Hannah.

"I played with great players and I coached quite a few as well," Berry said. "I don't know anyone who worked harder and got more out of himself on the field and in practice than John. It was a great privilege to coach him."

Hannah said he realized he was in the NFL during his rookie year when the Patriots lined up against the Chicago Bears and Dick Butkus was on the other side of the line of scrimmage. "It was his last year and he couldn't move around very well anymore," Hannah said. "But he could still pack a wallop. He hit harder than anyone I ever went up against. He was tough and nasty and if you could survive being on the field with Butkus you could survive going up against anyone."

Hannah also cited Bob Lilly, Randy White, Merlin Olsen, Howie Long, Joe Klecko, and Fred Smerlas among the toughest men he ever went up against. Interestingly, the Patriots and Oakland Raiders were known for their hatred of each other and for the win-at-all costs attitude both teams brought against each other. The origin of the disdain between the two teams dated back to the 1976 season, when the Patriots handed the Raiders their only regular-season defeat, a 48–17 demolition in New England in which the Raiders believed the Patriots "rubbed it in." The Raiders squeaked by the Pats that year in the divisional playoffs, 24–21, in a game that had several key controversial calls—including a roughing-the-passer penalty against Patriots defensive lineman Ray "Sugar Bear" Hamilton during Oakland's game-winning drive.

Despite this open animosity, when the Raiders' Long went up against Hannah, it was anything but dirty. Both future Hall of Famers went after each other hard but kept it clean.

"That was John Hannah," Long said. "As far as I'm concerned there was a real respect factor there. He was one of the greatest offensive linemen ever and that's the way he played."

#22

GALE SAYERS

There are many sportswriters who would not include Gale Sayers on a list of the 165 greatest players in pro-football history, let alone the top 65. Forgive me for being blunt, but those people are simply ignorant.

Sayers's career was short (shorter even than Earl Campbell's). Sayers began in the NFL in 1965 and was done by the end of the 1971 season. Knee injuries ripped his career apart. However, he was a comet that flew over the NFL with remarkable running skills that would have made him the best at his position in many eras. Perhaps Jim Brown had more overall talent and perhaps Barry Sanders was more elusive. However, if you put all three of them in the same training camp and had to give the job to one of them, Sayers may very well have won that competition.

The Chicago Bears' George Halas drafted Sayers in 1965 and knew that he had something special when he watched his college films from Kansas. Halas had been basically the driving force behind the NFL when it came into existence 45 years earlier. His barnstorming tour with Red Grange in 1925 gave pro football the credibility it was lacking and helped start the NFL on its way toward becoming the most successful sports league ever. Halas looked at Sayers and compared him to Grange.

The comparison couldn't have been more correct. Grange was explosively fast in his heyday, quick as a hiccup, and simply exploded into the secondary any time he could find daylight. Four decades after the Galloping Ghost's Bears debut, Sayers established himself as a superstar as a rookie by scoring six touchdowns in one game on a rainy afternoon against the San Francisco 49ers on December 12, 1965. He had 336 all-purpose yards in the 61–20 rout. NFL Films used that game to get the inside story on Sayers and they captured the running back's essence on the field when he explained what he needed to be successful. "Just give me 18 inches of daylight," Sayers said without a hint of a smile. "That's all I need."

Sayers's six-touchdown performance—tying a mark set by Ernie Nevers of the Chicago Cardinals against Halas's Bears in 1929—was remarkable because it came on a field that was in miserable condition because of the rain. Most of the players were slipping and sliding and that made tackling Sayers a major issue. But for some reason, Sayers seemed comfortable on the muddy field. Sayers had TD runs of 21, 7, 50, and 1 yards. He also scored on an 80-yard reception on a screen pass and on an 85-yard punt return. "I never thought about what the weather was like or what the field was like," Sayers said. "I just thought about doing my job. I wanted to run with the ball and score if possible. On that day every time I looked up there was a lane to the end zone."

Gale Sayers

The Bears had a mediocre offensive line in those days yet Sayers still scored a league-leading 22 total touchdowns as a rookie despite being the center of attention every time he stepped onto the football field. The extra attention didn't bother Sayers at all. "I don't care how many of the defensive players are trying to key on me," Sayers explained. "They can only put 11 men on the field and they can all look at me. They have to tackle me and that's the issue."

Sayers's ability to start, get to full speed, stop, and cut in a heartbeat was thrilling to Halas. "Gale detects daylight," Halas said. "The average back, when he sees a hole, will try to bull his way through. But Gale, if the hole is even partly clogged, instinctively takes off in the right direction. And he does it so swiftly and surely that the defense is usually frozen."

Like Barry Sanders, Sayers could not always explain his methods. But he could explain his game plan. "If they think they know where I am going, that's fine," Sayers explained. "But when they get to the spot they think I'm going to be, I will not be there at that moment."

Sayers suffered the first of two devastating knee injuries in a 1968 game against the San Francisco 49ers when defensive back Kermit Alexander hit him in the right knee and tore ligaments. If the injury had happened a couple of generations later, Sayers would have had arthroscopic surgery and returned in nearly the same condition he was in before the damage had been done. Instead, Sayers didn't return until 1969 and the injury had left him more of power back than the unique talent who could run like the wind and find the opening in the defense.

Sayers didn't give up or complain that the injury had robbed him of his unique talent, though. Instead, he ran for 1,032 yards and eight touchdowns as he bowled tacklers over and created shocking force when he hit them.

Sayers was in the process of making his transition from speed back to power back and he was doing a good job at it. Then he tore ligaments in his left knee in a 1970 preseason game and that was basically it for his career. He worked to rehab but he could no longer bring it the way he had before the injury.

As a result, Sayers had to retire after the 1971 season having amassed 4,956 career rushing yards, an average of 5.0 yards per carry and 39 rushing touchdowns. He added nine more scores as a receiver, six as a kickoff returner, and two as a punt returner. He even threw a touchdown pass when the Bears asked him to throw the option pass. There wasn't a thing Sayers was incapable of doing on the football field and he knows that injuries kept him from doing more. "I would have played for many more years had I had that opportunity," Sayers said. "I think my numbers would have been much more memorable had I been able to continue to run the way I could have when I first came up."

There's little doubt that Sayers's assessment was right on.

#23

DAN MARINO

Every year at draft time quarterbacks are at the center of most discussions. Scouts, analysts, coaches, and other experts discuss the qualities needed to excel at the most important position. Factors like accuracy, release, and decision making ability are examined ad nauseam. Then, when talk turns to arm strength, the subject is usually downplayed.

"It seems they don't like to give a lot of credit to the quarterbacks with the strongest arms," said Fox analyst Jimmy Johnson, who coached the Dallas Cowboys to two Super Bowl titles. "But here's what you have to know: A quarterback with arm strength can turn a nothing play into a big play in an instant. The quarterback who is mobile and can read defenses but doesn't have that velocity can't do that."

No quarterback ever threw the football with more velocity than Dan Marino. Many of the other great quarterbacks of his era—Joe Montana, Steve Young, Troy Aikman, and Phil Simms—give credit to Marino for having an absolute gun that could whistle the ball to the sidelines or deep down the field to receivers like Mark Clayton and Mark Duper (a.k.a. "The Marks Brothers") and give the Miami Dolphins an edge in big games.

Marino had tremendous arm strength but he also had the quickest release this side of Joe Namath. There must be something to the theory that if you want a quarterback you should go to western Pennsylvania to find him. Namath, Montana, Jim Kelly, and Johnny Unitas all spent their formative years in Western Pennsylvania, as did the redoubtable Marino.

The Dolphins were fortunate to get Marino in the great quarterback draft class of 1983. Marino was the No. 27 overall pick (the last of six quarterbacks chosen in the first round) and Miami head coach Don Shula couldn't have been more thrilled to get him. Before Marino had arrived in Miami, the Dolphins were a team that had a strong defense and a decent running game, but its passing game was just a rumor. With the strong-armed Marino lining up under center, Shula was convinced that he had another Super Bowl team to go with the titles he had won with quarterback Bob Griese in 1972 and '73. "He had everything you were looking for in a quarterback and I was not about to let him get by," Shula said. "I never thought we would get a chance to draft him. It was a great day when we made him a Dolphin."

Marino was eager to show the 26 teams that passed on him that they had made a regrettable mistake. If he had had a mediocre senior year at the University of Pittsburgh that caused his draft status to suffer, Marino was determined to get off to a quick start with the Dolphins. He was more than happy to put his gun on display as well as his quick release.

It was obvious in his first training camp that the Dolphins would no longer be a team content to play defense and run the ball. They would become a team that aired it out. There was little opposing teams could do when Marino got decent protection, a fact that was not lost on Hall of Fame defensive back Ronnie Lott.

"You were basically at Dan's mercy," said Lott. "All the great ones see the game so quickly that when everybody else is running around like a chicken with his head cut off, they know exactly where they want to go with the ball. It's like they see everything in slow motion.

"Then you also have the release and the arm strength. He knew the ins and outs of the game so well and then he could just put so much on the ball. He was one of a kind."

A nine-time Pro Bowl selection and the 1984 league MVP, Marino owned 22 different NFL passing records at the time of his retirement after the 1999 season. He led the league in completions six times, threw for 20 touchdowns or more in a season 13 times, had four TD passes or more in a game 21 times, and threw for 3,000 yards or more in a season 13 times.

In the 1984 season, Marino threw for a league record 5,084 passing yards and 48 touchdowns, shattering the previous record of 36 set by George Blanda and Y.A. Tittle. That touchdown mark has since been broken by Peyton Manning (49) and later by Tom Brady (50), but Marino's 1984 MVP season still stands as one of the greatest single-season performances in NFL history.

"What he accomplished is to have a better season than anyone who has ever played this game," said former Dallas quarterback Roger Staubach. "I'm talking about quarterbacks, wide receivers, or anyone else. He was unbelievable."

The Dolphins rolled to a 14–2 record that season and captured the AFC championship, setting up a Super Bowl showdown against the San Francisco 49ers. The glamorous matchup between Marino and Joe Montana was one of the most anticipated in Super Bowl history. After years of one-sided matchups, many thought Super Bowl XIX would be a high-scoring game that would come down to who had the ball last. In reality, it started out that way but the Dolphins could not keep up and the Niners walked away with a 38–16 win.

Unfortunately for Marino, that would be the only time he would get to compete in a Super Bowl. As the seasons rolled by, Marino felt the pain of never being part of a championship team. Critics and analysts always finished his career assessments by talking about the fact that Marino had never won a ring. Marino never denied that it hurt.

"I'd trade every record I have to have been a part of a championship team," Marino said. It's not like it was Marino's fault. The great defense the Dolphins had when he came to the team out of Pittsburgh disappeared. As the years went by, Marino had to throw the ball in order to help the Dolphins compete in most games. The defense regularly failed in big games, giving up an average of 44.5 points in 10 playoff defeats. That was clearly not a problem caused by Marino. He was left to cope with a poor defense and he was not able to do it all by himself.

But that doesn't mean he didn't have the best arm of anyone who ever played the game.

MOST 400-YARD GAMES BY A QUARTERBACK (THROUGH 2008 SEASON)		
Quarterback	**Team**	**400-Yard Games**
1. Dan Marino	MIA	13
2. Peyton Manning	IND	7
Joe Montana	SF-KC	7
Warren Moon	HOU-MIN-SEA-KC	7
5. Drew Bledsoe	NE-BUF-DAL	6
Dan Fouts	SD	6
7. Sonny Jurgensen	PHI-WSH	5
Dave Krieg	SEA-KC-DET-AZ-CHI-TEN	5

"CLASS OF 1983" FIRST-ROUND QUARTERBACKS IN COMPARISON (IN DRAFT ORDER)

	Years	Att	Comp	Yards	TD	Int	W–L–T	Drafted by
John Elway	1983–1998	7,250	4,123	51,475	300	226	148–82–1	DEN
Todd Blackledge	1983–1989	881	424	5,286	29	38	15–14–0	KC
Jim Kelly	1986–1996	4,779	2,874	35,467	237	175	101–59–0	BUF*
Tony Eason	1983–1990	1,564	911	11,142	61	51	28–23–0	NE
Ken O'Brien	1984–1993	3,602	2,110	25,094	128	98	50–59–1	NYJ
Dan Marino	1983–1999	8,358	4,967	61,361	420	252	147–93–0	MIA

*Played in USFL (1984–85)

#24

OTTO GRAHAM

The leather helmet without bars. The jumping-pass poses arranged by photographers. Otto Graham couldn't possibly have played the same game that Joe Montana, Johnny Unitas, and Peyton Manning played, could he?

There were none of the same trappings around pro football in the 1940s and '50s that exist today. It wasn't an event to go to a game on a Sunday afternoon. Players weren't lionized because they were good enough to play for pay. No, they were just doing a job.

Graham, as the quarterback of the Cleveland Browns, did his job remarkably well. During his 10-year run as the Browns quarterback,

Graham led them to the championship game every year. They won seven of those title games.

When Graham lined up at quarterback, the Browns would win. Sometimes they would be blowouts and sometimes they would be close games, but the Waukegan, Illinois, native and Northwestern University graduate found a way to win football games. Stack all the top quarterbacks in the game and arrange them by winning percentage. Graham, who compiled a record of 105–17–4 during his decade in Cleveland stands on top of all of them.

Statistically, it is a different game today than it was in Graham's era. Today, quarterbacks regularly complete 62 to 67 percent of their passes and it is taken as a matter of course. But it wasn't always that way. Up through the late 1970s, if a quarterback completed 50 percent or more of his passes he was usually one of the better passers in the league. Graham was far better than that. During his career with the Browns—four were in the All-America Football Conference—his worst numbers came in 1952 when he completed 49.7 percent of his passes. However, it was not exactly a terrible year for Graham. He completed 181 of 364 passes for a career-high 2,816 with 20 touchdowns and 24 interceptions and the Browns won the NFL's American Conference before losing to the Detroit Lions in the NFL championship.

It was the next year that was truly amazing for Graham. He completed 167 of 258 passes for 2,722 yards, a 64.7 completion percentage. That kind of accuracy would be lauded today but back then it was simply off the charts—like Bob Beamon's 29-foot-2½ inch broad jump in the 1968 Mexico City Olympics. (Beamon's mark stood for 23 years before it was finally broken by Mike Powell in 1991.) No other starting quarterback completed better than 54 percent of his passes in 1953. Graham threw for 11 touchdowns and ran for six more as the Browns went 11–1. While they lost in the title game again to the Lions, 17–16, they made Detroit pay the following year with a 56–10 romp in the title game.

Graham's teammates knew they were playing with greatness. "I remember Otto as a truly great quarterback and a truly great leader," said Bill Willis, a Hall of Fame defensive lineman who played with Graham on the Browns from 1946 through 1953. "He was a real general on the football field. All of the guys respected him. Nobody talked in the huddle, unless he gave them permission. Being the outstanding player he was, he was just as outstanding a person. He never really bragged about his abilities, even though his abilities were so good. He was very personable in the locker room. On the field he was all business. He was the guy you wanted to have in the huddle when the game was on the line."

Nobody appreciated Graham more than his coach, Paul Brown. Gruff and demanding, Brown got more than he had ever hoped for with Graham. "The test of a quarterback is where his team finishes," Brown said. "By that standard, Otto was the best of them all."

Brown and Graham combined to form one of the most productive coach-player relationships in sports history. The Browns so dominated the AAFC—winning four consecutive titles, going undefeated in 1948 and setting all the league's attendance records—that the NFL could not ignore them any longer. The Browns and two other AAFC teams (the San Francisco 49ers and Baltimore Colts) joined the NFL prior to the start of the 1950 season. NFL commissioner Bert Bell knew a great promotion when he saw one, and he made the first game of the season a matchup between the Browns and the two-time defending NFL champion Philadelphia Eagles. It was eagerly anticipated by football fans throughout the country and the belief was that the powerful Eagles would hammer away at the supposedly inferior Browns. Instead, Graham and the Browns used their superior skill to embarrass the Eagles and the NFL in a 35–10 rout.

"That was the game I remember most," Graham said. "We were so fired up, we would've played them for a keg of beer or a chocolate milkshake."

Otto Graham

It was a remarkable win that validated not only the Browns but the other two AAFC teams that came into the NFL. Graham and the Browns would also bookend that performance at the end of the season. After going 10–2 during the year and tying the New York Giants for the American Conference title, they beat the Giants in a one-game playoff, 8–3, and then edged the Los Angeles Rams in the NFL championship game, 30–28. Graham threw four touchdown passes in the win over the Rams.

Graham's spectacular ability to lead his team into the championship game 10 straight years will always be his legacy; he only averaged 10 yards or more per attempt in three seasons. On the other hand, quarterback Sid Luckman reached that figure twice, Norm Van Brocklin achieved it twice, Sammy Baugh never reached it, nor did greats Benny Friedman, Bob Waterfield, and Y.A. Tittle. All of those quarterbacks, like Graham, are in the Hall of Fame.

Graham never missed a game due to injury in his career but a blow to the face in a 1953 game resulted in an awful cut inside his mouth that required 15 stitches to close. After that, he became the first player to wear a facemask on his helmet. He was as innovative off the field as he was productive on it, and Graham will always be remembered as the greatest winner in the game's history.

#25

MEL BLOUNT

It would be easy to look at the career of Pittsburgh Steelers cornerback Mel Blount and say that he was a good player who benefited from having stars such as Joe Greene, Jack Ham, Jack Lambert, and L.C. Greenwood playing in front of him on the defense. He did benefit from having those stars around, as well as a great defensive coordinator in Bud Carson designing the attacking style the Steelers put on display throughout the 1970s. But to call Blount a good player is like calling Iron Chef Mario Batali a decent cook.

Blount did not invent bump-and-run coverage by a cornerback—that honor belongs to Hall of Famer Willie Brown—but he did perfect it. Blount was a remarkable athlete who outleaped Olympic hurdler Renaldo Nehemiah while wearing street shoes and could outrun nearly everyone he ever encountered on the football field.

He looked the part of the world-class athlete, according to his teammates. "Size, speed, quickness, toughness, that's what Mel had," said former Steelers quarterback Terry Hanratty. "If you gave Blount free rein to hit you, you were in trouble because, if he missed, he had the speed to catch up. A lot of receivers got short arms when they were in Mel's territory."

As important as his athletic ability was, Blount was driven to be the best player on the field every time he put on a uniform.

"I didn't want to be second to anyone," he said. "I wanted to set the standards for my position."

Ham, who was one of the most gifted linebackers of his era, marveled at Blount's talent. "When you create a cornerback, the mold is Mel Blount," Ham said. "I played in a lot of Pro Bowls. I never saw a cornerback like him. He was the most incredible athlete I have ever seen. With Mel, you could take one wide receiver and just write him off. He could handle anybody in the league."

Blount was not an immediate success in the NFL, though. Coming from Southern University, he wasn't used to the mental game played in the NFL. Receivers could use his athletic ability against him and take advantage of him with double moves. However, once he decided to learn the nuances of the cornerback position he was a different player. "I was emotional and when I got beaten I got upset," Blount recalled. "But once I got to my first offseason, I realized that when someone beat me it was just a chance for me to learn a lesson. I studied every play and learned what happened. And I talked with Bud and I listened to everything he said. It seemed to work."

It all started to come together in the 1972 season, when Blount did not get beaten for a touchdown all year. Three years later, he was named the Most Valuable Defensive Player by the Associated Press, becoming the first cornerback to earn this award. Blount had

57 interceptions as well as 13 fumble recoveries in a career that earned him five trips to the Pro Bowl.

But numbers don't tell the story of Blount's career. They may show that he could turn games around with his ability to pick off the ball and demonstrate good hands, but it was the fire he brought when covering and tackling that was his signature. As he came to understand the way NFL offenses attacked, it basically became no contest. He was sharper mentally than almost all of his opponents and his physical edge allowed him to dominate. He frequently ate up star receivers like Fred Biletnikoff, Isaac Curtis, and Cliff Branch.

Blount's bump-and-run coverage was so effective that the NFL came to a conclusion that defensive dominance was not good for the game. As a result, rules were changed and Blount was no longer allowed to bump receivers after they got past the five-yard mark.

While Steelers head coach Chuck Noll cried about the rule change, Blount simply changed his tactics and adjusted. He started playing the trail technique in which he let the receiver get ahead of him and then would turn on the speed that would allow him to come in and steal the pass or deflect it away.

Blount's hunger was probably the key to his long-term success on the field. He was one of the toughest practice players to ever wear a Steelers uniform and he honed his skills by going up against Hall of Famers Lynn Swann and John Stallworth in practice every day. He took it personally if either receiver ever caught a pass against him in a scrimmage.

Blount was driven to be successful every time he took the field. He didn't want anybody to catch a pass against him and that was his motivation throughout his 14-year career. "If the scales were balanced, there was nobody I couldn't cover," he said. "That's what motivated me, drove me to be as good as I was. I was in front of 50,000 people in the stands and millions on TV. I didn't want to be embarrassed."

That almost never happened to Blount.

#26

DEION SANDERS

As great a player as Deion Sanders was in the National Football League—he was a 10-time All-Pro performer—he could have been even better had he committed to football full-time. Instead, Sanders also pursued a baseball career and was good enough to last nine seasons in the major leagues.

There is little doubt that Sanders was one of the best athletes to ever play the game. When it came to the particular job of covering receivers, many NFL scouts, coaches, and general managers believe Sanders was the best ever. Sanders did not invent the term, but after he was drafted by the Atlanta Falcons in 1989, head coach Jerry Glanville (who came aboard the following year) said the team's confidence was so strong in Sanders that they would simply "leave him on the island" against the opponent's best receiver. That phrase has since become part of the NFL's daily lexicon when it comes to a cornerback who can cover a receiver without any help.

Sanders came into the league referring to himself as "Prime Time" and boasting extreme confidence in his abilities. He didn't think he would have any kind of adjustment period after his career at Florida State came to an end and the Falcons called his name with the fifth pick in the draft. "I have watched the NFL and they have talented receivers," Sanders said. "But what do I have to be afraid of? Are they faster than I am? Are they more talented than I am? I don't think so. From what I see, they have a lot more to be fearful of than I do. Go ahead and call me cocky or arrogant. But I'm being honest. I don't see why I should have trouble covering the NFL receivers."

This included San Francisco's Jerry Rice, the greatest receiver in NFL history. While Sanders did not win every battle against him, Rice realized that when he had to face Sanders it was going to be a major test of his abilities. Rice never lost any of his confidence when he was going up against Sanders, but he prepared differently for him than he did other defensive backs. "He was so fast and he had so much ability that you couldn't just go out and run against him," Rice recalled. "I studied him and tried to learn his tendencies. I know that's usually what defensive backs do, but when I had to go up against Deion or Darrell Green, I studied them. You have to get an edge somehow and that's what I would do."

Sanders put together remarkable numbers that spoke to his remarkable ability to turn a game around with his spectacular ability. Nine of his 53 regular-season interceptions were returned for touchdowns during his career, tied for second-best all-time. His career-high for interceptions in a single season was seven (1993) and that number is striking because it's not higher. One reason it isn't is because Sanders was so dominant in coverage that many teams wouldn't even test him. They would simply try their luck with one of the other Falcons defensive backs—remember the luckless Charles Dimry?—and simply not even look at Sanders' side of the ball. They knew he was too good to challenge.

Sanders always said that was one of the reasons he was interested in baseball. "I got bored sometimes," Sanders said. "They wouldn't throw to me or come to my side of the field. That leads to being bored."

Sanders got quite a bit of excitement from returning kickoffs and punts, though. Glanville wanted to get Sanders as many touches as he could, so he had Sanders return kicks—especially when the game was on the line. He had six punt returns and three kickoff returns for touchdowns in his career and was considered the most dangerous return man in the league for much of his career. His 19 total non-offensive touchdowns stand as a league record.

Sanders's game did have one glaring deficiency, though. From the time he was a college star at Florida State through his pro career with the Falcons, San Francisco 49ers, Dallas Cowboys, and Baltimore Ravens, he was never one who was going to stick his nose in the fray and make a big tackle. As the years went by his tendency to shy away from the physical contact became more and more pronounced. It was clear that Sanders did not enjoy that part of the game—when he was asked to evaluate his tackling, he said it was "lousy."

That part of his game made many of his coaches ill. But it also speaks to how good he was in coverage. It was impossible to shake Sanders with a single move, and double moves only created the illusion that a receiver was open. "They might be able to get a half-step but that was a good thing," Sanders explained. "I wanted the quarterback to think the receiver was open so he would throw to him and I could run in and get the interception. For someone to actually beat me, it had to be somebody like Jerry Rice or someone who ran the best route of his life. I was not about to let somebody say they got the best of Prime Time."

Sanders was enamored with self-promotion and getting his name in the headlines. That kind of behavior did not make him one of the game's most popular players. "There were fans who loved me and there were fans who hated me," Sanders said. "There were players who felt the same way. I was aware of that. But I was just going to be me the whole way through. I played the way I thought the game should be played and I was going to dance after an interception or a big play. If somebody didn't like it all they had to do was tackle me."

Sanders won back-to-back Super Bowls with the 49ers and Cowboys in 1994 and 1995. He called those moments the highlights of his career and it validated him as a team player. However, it was Sanders the individual who impressed fans the most. Running with an interception was his forte and he had 303 interception return yards in 1994 when he was with the Niners. Sanders's signature move was putting his hand on his helmet and then high-stepping into the end zone—with the cameras focusing on him and his opponents seething.

NON-OFFENSIVE TOUCHDOWN LEADERS (THROUGH 2013 SEASON)			
Rank	Player	Years	TDs
1	Deion Sanders	1989-2005	19
1	Devin Hester	2006-2013	19
3	Rod Woodson	1987-2003	17
4	Ronde Barber	1997-2012	14
5	Brian Mitchell	1990-2003	13
5	Lemar Parrish	1970-1982	13
5	Aeneas Williams	1991-2004	13
5	Darren Sharper	1997-2010	13
5	Charles Woodson	1998-2013	13
10	Eric Metcalf	1989-2002	12
10	Ken Houston	1967-1980	12
10	Dante Hall	2000-2008	12

#27

JIM PARKER

Jim Parker was one of the main reasons Johnny Unitas was able to become the greatest quarterback of his time. He was also one of the reasons that Lenny Moore became one of the most versatile running backs in the history of the game.

Parker came to the Baltimore Colts out of Ohio State as a magnificent run blocker but he did not know a lot about pass blocking. It didn't take him long to learn what his job was all about. "Weeb Ewbank pulled me aside and he pointed at Johnny," Parker recalled after he was named to the NFL's All-Century team. "'That's the man you have to protect. He has to stay on his feet and we don't want him hit.'

"I told him that I knew that already. He looked at me and said, 'Good, we shouldn't have any problems.'"

Parker knew his priority and he became one of the finest pass blockers the game had ever seen. Fueling his desire to protect Unitas and keep him from getting hurt was a genuine affection for the quarterback. "Here's the interesting thing," Parker said. "From the moment I got to Baltimore and met John Unitas, I could tell he was something special. I'm not talking about as a quarterback. That was pretty obvious from everything I saw on the practice field. But as a person. He was so genuine and so tough. He could take the most hellacious shot and get up and throw it 40 yards on a line. He gave it his all and that's the kind of person he was. He was a great person and a great teammate. You feel that way about somebody and you don't want anything to happen to him—especially on your watch."

Parker was the most versatile of blockers. He played for 11 years in Baltimore and was named to the All-Pro team eight times. He made it at guard four times and at tackle four other times. Parker was the biggest man the Colts had ever drafted when he was selected with the eighth overall pick in 1957. He stood 6-foot-3 and weighed 273 pounds—nearly unheard of size at that time. He had played on both lines at Ohio State and many pro scouts felt that Parker was better suited to defense. But Ewbank saw Parker's quick feet, his strong hands, and his overall awareness made him better suited to become a great blocker.

"It was all about protecting John and opening holes for Lenny," Parker recalled. "I knew if I could do those things that my time in Baltimore would work out fairly well."

Parker started out at tackle because he was big, strong, and fast enough to handle the best pass rushers in the game. Later on his career, Ewbank saw that Parker might be an even better guard because he had become such a great technician. He switched Parker to guard midway through the 1962 season and at the end of the year, he was named an All-Pro at both positions. He was named to the All-Pro team at guard from 1963 through 1965 as well.

There was no wasted movement or energy with Parker. Everything was done to keep the pass rusher out of the backfield or open a bigger running lane. He used his body to slam defensive linemen to the ground and to shield the skill-position players.

"He would never miss an opportunity to drive somebody into the ground," said former Colts center Buzz Nutter. "He really seemed to get real delight in getting a chance to run over some linebacker or defensive lineman. If he had a chance to take a step before he hit somebody it was no contest."

Parker was a dominant player for Woody Hayes at Ohio State and quickly adjusted to the NFL. He loved his job and he quickly set an overpowering goal for himself. "I didn't tell anyone but I knew I wanted to be known as the best blocker that ever played the game," Parker explained. "It was nothing I ever talked about when I was playing. To say something like that in public would not have been very smart. But once I got to the end of my career I could talk about it. I gave it everything I had."

Parker's ability was evident to his teammates from his first training camp in 1957. The Colts knew they had a team that had plenty of talent and had a chance to become contenders. But there was a certain lack of physical play that had kept them from becoming an elite team

"We were a good team and we knew we should be better," said former Colts receiver Raymond Berry. "But we were missing that guy who could help us when we had to go up against a big, tough, physical guy. For example, when we played the Bears, a guy like Doug Atkins would kill us. We couldn't handle him and there were a few others like that. But it all changed when Jim came here."

Once Parker was inserted at tackle, Atkins and other pass rushers were no longer factors. Atkins grew frustrated by Parker's consistency and tried to get under his skin by cursing at him. "I tried to get him off his game and nothing ever worked," Atkins said. "There were a few times I was able to hit him when I was running at full speed . . . and I couldn't even budge him. That's how strong he was and that's how tough he was."

Parker came up with one of his best performances in the Colts' 1958 NFL championship game against the New York Giants. The game would go on to be considered the greatest of all-time and Parker had to face Giants All-Pro defensive end Andy Robustelli. The Giants defense was dominant and Robustelli beat Parker on a couple of plays in the first quarter. However, that was it. Parker handled Robustelli the rest of the game.

Robustelli called Parker the "best offensive tackle I ever played against."

It was a label that many of the league's best defensive linemen concurred with during the late 1950s and 1960s.

#28

BRUCE SMITH

There was only one place Bruce Smith was going to end up after he ended his career with the Washington Redskins in 2003, and that was the Pro Football Hall of Fame in Canton, Ohio. It was a no-doubter since Smith finished his career with 200 sacks, putting him first on the official list of all-time sack leaders.

But the numbers don't tell the full story with Smith. Yes, he would get to the quarterback with frequency. But what he did during the week was force opposing offensive coordinators to account for him on every play and they still couldn't stop him—or even come close. In so doing, Smith's prowess opened up pass rush angles for Buffalo Bills teammates like Darryl Talley and Cornelius Bennett on the Bills defense. He was the dominant stud on a defensive team that was loaded with playmakers and he was nearly the equivalent of Reggie White.

But it almost didn't happen for the first overall pick in the 1985 NFL draft out of Virginia Tech, as Smith was saddled with a know-nothing head coach in Hank Bullough for the majority of his first two seasons with the Bills. At the time, Smith was not the dynamic 285-pound missile who rushed the passer from his right defensive end position for the majority of his career. His build was more similar to that of Baby Huey, the rotund cartoon duck who was in anything but good shape. The 1985 season was a banner year for the Chicago Bears, not the Buffalo Bills. The Bears used a rotund rookie of their own in William "The Refrigerator" Perry to see spot duty on Buddy Ryan's defensive line and to serve as a smashing power back in the Bears' offense. Bullough decided to let Smith follow the same route and said he thought "Smith could do for us what Perry did for the Bears."

It's a good thing for Smith, the Bills, and their fans that owner Ralph Wilson fired Bullough nine games into the 1986 season and replaced him with Marv Levy. The team would turn it around under Levy's leadership as he handed the offense over to Jim Kelly and focused the defense around Smith. The move would allow the Bills to become the dominant team in the AFC and much of it was due to Smith, who took the promotion seriously, got himself into remarkable condition, and became the most artistic pass rusher the game had ever seen.

Smith had an array of moves and lightning speed. What made him artistic was his ability to combine the two and just obliterate opposing tackles. "I knew there were some tackles out there who could contend with speed and some who knew how to counter moves, but if I could combine the two that would make things awfully tough," Smith explained. "There was a lot of hard work involved but it was all worth it because my teammates believed in me and so did my coaches."

Bruce Smith

The Bills would eventually make it to the Super Bowl four straight times in the early 1990s and infamously lose all four of them. They had their best team and their best chance in Super Bowl XXV when they faced the New York Giants in Tampa, Florida. The Bills were a high-scoring juggernaut that season and were coming off an AFC Championship Game in which they had obliterated the Los Angeles Raiders, 51–3. Smith was involved in one of the key plays in the Super Bowl when he came around the corner and sacked Giants quarterback Jeff Hostetler in the end zone for a second-quarter safety. The remarkable aspect to the play was that Hostetler held on to the ball as Smith delivered a karate chop with his right arm just as the Giants quarterback was bringing the ball into a passing position. Hostetler could easily have dropped the ball and Smith or one of his teammates could have fallen on it for a touchdown instead of a safety.

"That's football but it still was a shock to me that Hostetler did not lose that ball," Levy said. "Bruce came with such speed and so much pressure and force that it really was a remarkable play on his part not to fumble the ball and not to give us a touchdown. I know Bruce was shocked and my guess is that Hostetler was a little bit shocked that he held on to the ball."

The 1990 season was probably the best of Smith's career. He had a career-best 19 sacks and from that point on through the next seven seasons, Smith would be double-teamed on almost every play. His speed, strength and skill made that move almost moot. "I welcomed the double-team," said Smith. "They don't double-team guys who can't play. It was a sign of respect and it just made me play that much harder. I was determined to beat that double-team before that second guy came in, because I knew it was coming. It was just a matter of the lineman turning his head for that split second, and I was gone. Usually, the second guy was reaching for me, because I'd beaten the first guy so quick[ly]."

Smith, for his part, believes that he was the best defensive end to ever play the game. He knows that White has a lot of supporters as does Deacon Jones, but he refuses to take any kind of backseat. "I'm not saying that I'm the best defensive end pass rusher to play the game just because I'm the NFL all-time sack leader," he said, "but because of the degree of difficulty I had to overcome to achieve that feat."

Smith said that playing in a 3–4 defense throughout the majority of his career and having so much responsibility against the run made his job tougher than any other defensive lineman's. Smith's determination made blocking him against the run an exhaustive process. Normally, offensive tackles block speedy defensive ends to the outside and the running backs cut inside the defensive end to make their yardage. But Smith's quickness allowed him to catch and bring down the running back unless the tackle was able to sustain that block throughout the play.

"I don't remember that happening too many times," Smith said. "I could spin off the block and I could throw the tackle aside," Smith explained. "To block me for more than the initial surge was almost impossible."

Smith was always straight-forward and blunt in the Bills' locker room. "There was not much modesty to his game," Levy said. "He would tell you he was the best. But what made him special is that it wasn't just bluster. He would go out and prove it nearly every week. He was a very special player and I believe he was the best defensive end in the history of the game."

Smith's 200 sacks, 43 forced fumbles, 15 fumble recoveries, and 1,078 tackles make a strong case in his favor.

Bruce Smith

SACKS LEADERS

Player	Team	Years	No.
1. Bruce Smith	Buff.-Wash.	19	200
2. Reggie White	Phil.-GB	15	198
3. Kevin Greene	L.A. Rm.-Pitt.-Car.-SF-Car.	15	160
4. Chris Doleman	Minn.-Atl.-SF-Minn.	15	150.5
5. Michael Strahan	NYG	15	141.5
6. Jason Taylor	Mia.-Wash.-NYJ	15	139.5
7. Richard Dent	Chi.-SF-Chi.-Ind.-Phil.	15	137.5
John Randle	Minn.-Sea.	14	137.5
9. John Abraham	NYJ-Atl.-Ariz.	14	133.5
10. Lawrence Taylor	NYG	13	132.5
Leslie O'Neal	SD-STL-KC	13	132.5
10. Rickey Jackson	New Orleans	15	128

#29

MERLIN OLSEN

To millions of TV viewers, Merlin Olsen was the thoughtful TV analyst who came into your living room every Sunday in order to give fans insight on the game within the game. To millions more, he was one of the leads on *Little House on the Prairie* or *Father Murphy*. It's fair to say that a lot more fans remember Olsen for his work on the small screen than they do for his work on the football field— which is a shame because it was shockingly good.

Olsen was a huge piece of the Los Angeles Rams' legendary "Fearsome Foursome" defense, with Deacon Jones, Rosey Grier, and Lamar Lundy. Jones, of course, was the lead dog and the monster pass rusher who invented the term "sack" and was a garrulous presence with the media. Jones was one of the game's all-time greats (see No. 8) but the truth of the matter is that Olsen was nearly as good.

Olsen was one of the most consistent players the game has ever seen. He made the Pro Bowl 14 straight seasons between 1962 and 1975 (a record he shares with offensive lineman Bruce Matthews) and he played the game with a fierceness that belied his onscreen personality. "When the ball was snapped there was nothing gentle about Merlin Olsen," said Jones, speaking of his linemate's gentle-giant image. "No, he played hard every snap he was on the field and he was just a great teammate to have. He could rush the passer, stop the run and fill any gap that came along."

Many of those gaps were filled when Olsen was filling Jones's space, as Deacon would often loop to the outside so he could rush the quarterback. Olsen would move over from his defensive tackle position, handle his own responsibilities, and handle Jones's as well. That's the way Rams coaches George Allen and Chuck Knox wanted Olsen to play and that's just how he did it.

Olsen had dominant strength and quickness but what allowed him to make the All-NFL team first or second team 10 times was his intelligence. "I wanted to get better each and every year," Olsen said. "I was very concerned about correcting whatever was done incorrectly and doing it better. I was very concerned about who I was playing and what they were likely to do on the field so I could do my job better."

That study allowed Olsen to diagnose what was going on in the other huddle as if he had placed a microphone on the quarterback and put a listening device in his own ear. Most teams would use a screen pass or a draw play in order to suck the defensive playmakers out of position. That simply could not be done with Olsen, who knew what was going on almost before it happened and then would flow to the ball carrier so smoothly that the play would be over before it started.

While Olsen played hard every game and every down and had an inner fire that fueled him, he quickly realized that running backs and receivers were usually a lot more emotional in their pursuit of a big play or a touchdown than he was. While some may have viewed that as a flaw, Olsen looked at it as a strength because while they were pumping their fists and slapping high fives, Olsen was getting inside their heads and figuring out what they were doing. "Football linemen are motivated by a more complicated, self-determining series of factors than the simple fear of humiliation in the public gaze, which is the emotion that galvanizes the backs and receivers," Olsen said. "You could count on seeing your opponents getting themselves psyched up and taking an attitude that they could not be beaten on the field. Well, they could be beaten and it usually had to do with preparation, correct position and using the proper technique. Those things were great equalizers in the battle against emotion."

The mental game was Olsen's primary domain, but he could also get after the passer. He played in a time before sacks became an official statistic but he recorded 94 unofficial tallies in his 14-year career. He was happy to get them but only in the context that it helped the Rams defense and it helped the team win. "It was not about the glory that comes your way when you get the quarterback," Olsen said. "It was only about doing your job and doing what was expected in order to help the team. At the moment you are committed to getting to the passer and you know there's an opening, you explode into it and make the play happen. It's really a great feeling. I didn't get that feeling as often as [Deacon Jones] did, but I got it enough to know that it was a pretty wonderful feeling."

That cerebral approach also came into play when Olsen would assess his own play and realize he could have done things better. "One of life's most painful moments comes when we must admit that we didn't do our homework, that we are not prepared," Olsen said.

That may have been the ultimate secret to Olsen's success. While others were quick to recognize him and give him kudos, he was always tough on himself and demanded better. In reality, he was at the top for 14 years and his consistency provided the base of a superbly productive career.

#30

FORREST GREGG

Anyone who wins the Vince Lombardi derby is going to be in the top 65. Lombardi, one of the greatest coaches ever in any sport, had one favorite player—and it wasn't Paul Hornung. Lombardi loved the running back and thought he was a great guy in the locker room, but he had more respect for Forrest Gregg than any of his other players.

Considering that Lombardi had Bart Starr, Willie Davis, Jim Taylor, Ray Nitschke, and Willie Wood, that's quite a compliment. "Forrest Gregg was simply the finest player I ever coached," Lombardi said.

Lombardi, who had been an offensive lineman at Fordham during his college career and was one of the school's legendary

"Seven Blocks of Granite," had a soft spot in his heart for undersized offensive linemen. That's what he was and that's what Gregg was when he anchored the Green Bay Packers offensive line. At 6-foot-4 and 249 pounds, Gregg was not considered big for his position, yet he kept pass rushers at bay because he had the quickest feet of any offensive lineman of his time. He also possessed a sense of tenacity that coaches want from their tackles but seldom see to the level that Gregg could provide.

Gregg was in Green Bay throughout Lombardi's tenure and saw the team get better after a horrible season in 1958. The Packers went 1–10–1 under Ray "Scooter" McLean, but the team had the underpinnings of a decent offense with Bart Starr, Hornung, fullback Jim Taylor, tight end Max McGee, receiver Boyd Dowler, and another good blocker in Jerry Kramer. But Lombardi was taken by the blocking talents of Gregg, who had been used at guard by McLean.

Lombardi saw a nearly unbeatable tackle in Gregg and demanded only the best from him. Lombardi, whose legendary emotion invoked fear from nearly every player, saw that Gregg was just a bit more secure and a little more mature than most players. Gregg was unafraid of Lombardi's outbursts and the coach soon adopted Gregg as an ally in the locker room.

That first season in Green Bay (1959) turned out to be vital for Lombardi as the Packers went 7–5 and finished tied for third in the Western Conference. Hornung and Taylor continued to make progress and Gregg turned out to be the dominant blocker at tackle that Lombardi had envisioned before taking the head job in Green Bay. Hornung, Taylor, and Starr knew that Gregg could handle his matchup no matter who he was playing against and that confidence turned out to be one of the key ingredients for the Packers' growth to five-time NFL champion.

Gregg was anything but a superstar in his demeanor and considered himself a working man just doing his job. He knew, however, that he had come of age when he was able to hold his own against Baltimore Colts defensive end Gino Marchetti and Los Angeles Rams defensive end Deacon Jones in the early 1960s. Marchetti was a powerful pass rusher with plenty of athleticism, while Jones was a rookie with shocking quickness. Jones would later add the strength and moves that he would become famous for, but he was by far the quickest player in the league at his position at that time.

"Gino Marchetti was the best pass rusher I ever had to block and Deacon Jones was the quickest," Gregg said. "If you could hold your own against Marchetti you knew you were doing your job well. He had everything you wanted in a defensive end and he was kind of mean. Jones was just so fast that you couldn't believe how quick he could get out of his stance and up to full speed. He was the kind of guy who could test you on every snap. You felt good when you finished the game against the Rams with a win and you could get off the field and not have to stop him one more time."

In the 1960 season, the Packers beat the Rams in the season finale to win the Western Conference and go into the NFL Championship Game against the Philadelphia Eagles with the momentum of having won their last three games. But the Packers lost that championship game, the first and only postseason game that Lombardi ever lost.

Gregg, who went on to coach the Cleveland Browns, Cincinnati Bengals, and Packers, was taking notes. He saw how his coach prepared and how he got his players ready. He noticed how fine-tuned the Packers were in future championship games against the New York Giants, Browns, and Dallas Cowboys, and in Super Bowl wins over the Kansas City Chiefs and Oakland Raiders. "I don't think that it was any coincidence that we were at our best in most of those games," Gregg said. "Coach Lombardi always got us ready."

The Packers ground game operated at peak efficiency in those games and almost always rode the inside shoulder of Gregg at right tackle to get their famed power sweep going. "The guards did a lot of work on those sweeps, but so did Forrest," said Starr. "It was simple but it was beautiful to be a part of it. To see the blocking develop and to watch them execute was so gratifying. Give Paul [Hornung] and Jim [Taylor] credit as well because they were running the ball. But the coordination of the blockers made it go."

Gregg never asked for glory but he earned it on an every-game basis. He was a technician who operated at peak efficiency and had five championship rings to show for it. If there was ever any chance of remaining in the background, it was put away forever when Lombardi made his declaration.

#31

KELLEN WINSLOW

Coaches clamor for a tight end who can go up the seam, blow by the defensive back, and make a big play downfield. It's safe to say this idea was mere fantasy before Kellen Winslow came on the scene in 1979. Winslow was one of the first great athletes to play the tight-end position and no coach knew how to take advantage of his talent better than coach Don Coryell, who drafted him in San Diego and made him a centerpiece of the Chargers' offense.

The fact that Winslow had the brilliant Dan Fouts throwing to him helped his career develop. But it was Coryell who knew of Winslow's talent when he was a college tight end at Missouri and then saw him dominate in his first training camp with his remarkable athletic ability.

But calling Winslow a great athlete is not meant to slight him as a player who worked on his skills every day He could make the difficult catch in traffic and knew how to get the ball at its highest point. He made life much easier for Fouts whenever he needed to keep a drive alive. "Kellen knew how to get open and make plays when it mattered," Fouts said. "He could keep drives alive because he could make one quick move and get open. If he didn't get open he would fight for the ball and win the fight. When it mattered most he got the job done and, of course, he was really at his best in the biggest games."

Winslow's most heroic performance came in a 1981 playoff game between the Chargers and the Miami Dolphins. The Chargers won the battle in South Florida in overtime, 41–38, thanks to Winslow being virtually unstoppable. He caught 13 passes for 166 yards and blocked a Dolphins field goal attempt with four seconds remaining to send the game into the extra session. Winslow, who cramped up as the game progressed because of the high humidity in Miami, had to be helped from the Orange Bowl by his teammates—but not before he carried the Chargers on his back to a victory.

"That was the game that I'll be remembered for and I'm damn proud of what happened on the field that day," Winslow said. "I gave it everything I had and everyone on the field was going to do everything possible to keep our season alive. The circumstances were hard and we played a great team, but we found a way to win.

"It was the kind of game that you knew was really special as you were playing it. The way we started was shocking for them [the Chargers jumped to a 24–0 lead]. The way they came back was shocking for us. But then there was the back-and-forth of the game, the fans at the Orange Bowl, and the high drama. You knew it was one of the greatest games ever played and it was certainly the best game I ever played in."

Winslow's performance was obviously special, but the fact that Hall of Fame coach Don Shula singled him out after the game under such painful circumstances for the Dolphins has made that game live on in the minds of football fans who were at the rickety Orange Bowl or watched it on television. "He was Superman," Shula said. "Every time they needed a play there was Winslow catching the ball. We had no answers for him and it was just an unbelievable showing."

Winslow was the first tight end to put wide-receiver-type numbers together over the course of a season. Injuries held him down as a rookie as he caught only 25 passes. But in the 1980 season, he shocked the NFL by catching 89 passes for 1,290 yards and nine touchdowns. By the midway point of that season, opponents were game-planning to stop Winslow but they couldn't do it. The Chargers were a prolific offense with receivers Charlie Joiner and John Jefferson in addition to Winslow, so there was no way they could give full attention to Winslow. Prior to that season, opponents never fathomed the idea of covering a tight end with anything other than a linebacker or safety, but Winslow's skill set changed that. Opponents started to cover him with their cornerbacks, but that was hardly the answer either because he was just too big and strong for most of the cover men.

The 1980 season was a remarkable one for the high-powered "Air Coryell" offense as Winslow, Jefferson, and Joiner were the three leading receivers in the AFC and Fouts threw for 4,715 yards (a record he would break himself just one year later) and 30 touchdowns. "I don't think you'll ever see a team like that again," Fouts said. "To have one receiver who can dominate a game is one thing and to have two is just awesome. But to have three who can turn a game around gives an offense so many options. I think the fact that Kellen was such an original at his position probably made the biggest difference. Tight ends could not do what he did until Kellen came around and defenses didn't know how to deal with him. And even if they had figured it out we had other great receivers who could pick up the slack."

Winslow was a game-changing player in many ways. No tight end had ever caught the ball more than 75 times in a season before Winslow came along and Winslow caught 88 passes or more in three seasons out of four beginning in 1980. Winslow's pass catching talent allowed Coryell and a bright assistant coach named Joe Gibbs to re invent the tight end position. The Chargers did not have Winslow fulfill the normal tight end role of blocking, as he was too valuable as a receiver. As a result, Coryell and Gibbs came up with the two-tight end formation, a concept that Gibbs would take with him when he became the head coach of the Redskins in 1981.

Mike Ditka and John Mackey had been the standard bearers at the tight end position for the way they played in the 1960s. Until those two became pass-catching factors on an every-game basis, tight ends were largely blockers who would occasionally catch a pass as a safety valve from the quarterback. Those two redefined the position. Then Winslow came along and kicked it up a couple of levels. Despite great subsequent tight ends like Tony Gonzalez, Antonio Gates, and Shannon Sharpe, they are still following Winslow's lead.

RECEIVING LEADERS AMONG TIGHT ENDS (YARDAGE)

Rank	Player	Rec	Yds	Avg	TD
1	Tony Gonzalez	1325	15,127	11.4	111
2	Shannon Sharpe	815	10,060	12.3	62
3	Jason Witten	879	9,799	11.1	52
4	Antonio Gates	719	9,193	12.8	87
5	Ozzie Newsome	662	7,980	12.1	47
6	Jackie Smith	480	7,918	16.5	40
7	Kellen Winslow	541	6,741	12.5	45
8	Steve Jordan	498	6,307	12.7	28

#32

EMMITT SMITH

The 1990 draft marked one of those times the NFL forgot about suspending reality and the right thing actually happened.

In 1989, the Dallas Cowboys had drafted Troy Aikman, the premier quarterback available, with the first overall pick. Head coach Jimmy Johnson was bound and determined to get a running back able to carry the load and take some of the pressure off of his young quarterback. The Cowboys had the 21st pick in the following draft, and Johnson was very familiar with a back from the University of Florida named Emmitt Smith.

Johnson, who had been the head coach at the University of Miami when Smith was a record-setting high school running back at nearby Escambia (Fla.) High School, had tried to recruit Smith. He knew he had no chance because the Hurricanes featured a pro-style offense while the Florida Gators promised to use Smith as their featured back. Smith performed phenomenally well in college, and Johnson was hoping against hope that the great back would fall to him at the 21st pick. Johnson laughed at scouting reports knocked the 5-foot-9 Smith for being too small and too slow, because he had posted an unimpressive time of 4.7 seconds in the 40-yard dash at the draft combine.

"You would have had to be an idiot not to think Emmitt Smith was not going to be a great player," Johnson said. "I had seen enough of him as a high-school and college player to know that he was going to be a great one. However, when we did our background check on Emmitt, the things we hadn't known about him locked that pick up completely. He was the kind of player that left everything on the practice field. He played hurt. He always wanted the ball and he cared about doing the little things to win."

Johnson knew the 21st pick was not high enough to get Smith. So instead of staying put and going after defensive players, he traded up with the Pittsburgh Steelers so he could pick Smith with the 17th pick. Prior to making the pick, the phone rang in the Cowboys war room. The Atlanta Falcons had wanted the pick and proposed a trade, but Johnson refused to even consider it. "It's too late, we've made our pick," said Johnson. "We're taking Smith."

Smith held out through all of his first training camp, using owner Jerry Jones's words against him. Jones had called him the fourth-best player in the draft the night before the Cowboys selected him. Jones had wanted to pay him as the 17th-best player but Smith kept reminding Jones of his own words and eventually Jones met his price. After the long holdout, Smith became the Cowboys' starting running back the second game of his rookie season. However, Dallas was not using him the way they needed to. Midway through the season, Smith had only one 100-yard game, and the Cowboys appeared to be settling into a pattern where they were using him 10-to-15 times a game. Smith brought this to the attention of the coaching staff. "Every week in meetings, the coaching staff had come to the conclusion that we needed to gain 100 yards rushing in the game but they weren't giving me the ball," Smith said. "I let them know that and said I needed the ball to get 100 yards. They started to listen after that."

Smith went on to gain 937 yards and score 11 rushing touchdowns as a rookie—not exactly a legendary pace but enough to earn him AP offensive rookie of the year honors and to show the Cowboys that they needed to make him the focus of the game plan. Aikman was clearly a big-armed quarterback who could stretch the defense and wideout Michael Irvin was special as well, but neither could handle the primary role in the Cowboys offense the way Smith could.

The decision to give the ball to Smith paid big dividends after that. Smith led the league in rushing with 1,563 yards and 12 touchdowns in 1991 and continued to dominate with 1,713 yards and 18 touchdowns in 1992. The Cowboys rolled to the Super Bowl and beat the Buffalo Bills, 52–17. Yes, the Cowboys got great play from Aikman, Irvin, the offensive line, and the defense, but it was Smith who was dominating with his incessant pounding and relentless attack.

"That was Emmitt's outstanding quality," said Aikman. "The relentlessness, the determination, and the success. He was not going to allow the idea to enter his head that he wouldn't meet his goals and he wouldn't be successful. He was dominant and just about impossible to stop."

The success continued on an every-year basis. He rushed for 1,486 in 1993, capturing both league and Super Bowl MVP honors. He rushed for 1,484 yards in 1994 and an amazing 1,773 yards in 1995, posting 46 rushing touchdowns in that span, and giving the Cowboys a dominant ground game in an era when the pass was king. Feature stories were written by knowledgeable writers saying that Irvin was the most important of the Cowboys triplets because his ability kept defenses from focusing on Smith and stacking the defense against him. That argument had some validity, but the reality is that Johnson made Smith the focus of the game plan, when he left the team after a blowup with Jones, new head coach Barry Switzer did the exact same thing.

Smith was simply never satisfied and he was on pace to become the NFL's all-time leading rusher. His idol, Walter Payton of the Chicago Bears, was in his sights. Smith had always been goal-oriented but had done it within a team concept. He was getting his yardage and the Cowboys had won three championships. As the yards piled up, he was humbled by the idea of approaching Payton, who died in 1999 of a rare liver disease. When he passed Payton's all-time rushing record of 16,726 yards three years after Payton died, Smith was both joyous and tearful at the accomplishment. He gave a little point to the sky after an 11-yard run against the Seattle Seahawks that put him over the top. "For you, Walter," he said to himself.

He would go on to push the mark to 18,355 yards before retiring after the 2004 season. Today, five years after his retirement, Smith stands as not only the league's all-time leading rusher, but also the all-time leader in carries (4,409), touches (4,924), and rushing touchdowns (164). He is second all-time in both total touchdowns (175) and total yards from scrimmage (21,579). Not too bad for a guy considered to small and too slow to play in the NFL.

"I just wanted to do my job," Smith explained. "I never wanted anyone to say that Emmitt Smith wasn't giving everything he had. That was my bottom line."

RUSHING YARDS LEADERS (THROUGH 2013 SEASON)					
Rank	Running back	Years	Rushing yards	YPA	Rush YPG
1	Emmitt Smith	1990-2004	18,355	4.2	81.2
2	Walter Payton	1975-1987	16,726	4.4	88
3	Barry Sanders	1989-1998	15,269	5	99.8
4	Curtis Martin	1995-2005	14,101	4	83.9
5	LaDainian Tomlinson	2001-2011	13,684	4.3	80.5
6	Jerome Bettis	1993-2005	13,662	3.9	71.2
7	Eric Dickerson	1983-1993	13,259	4.4	90.8
8	Tony Dorsett	1977-1988	12,739	4.3	73.6
9	Jim Brown	1957-1965	12,312	5.2	104.3
10	Marshall Faulk	1994-2005	12,279	4.3	69.8

#33

DARRELL GREEN

Darrell Green didn't preen like Deion Sanders. Nor was he lionized like Rod Woodson or Mel Blount. However, when Green arrived with the Redskins in 1983, the 5-foot-8 cornerback from Texas A&I put his world-class speed on display and didn't stop for 20 years.

Green was simply one of the best cover men to ever play. His great speed was the key ingredient in his ability to shut down much bigger receivers but it was hardly his only asset. Green also had great hands, instincts and knew how to rise to the occasion in big moments.

Start with his first game of his NFL career in 1983. The Washington Redskins were playing their archrival Dallas Cowboys on a Monday night, and the formidable Tony Dorsett was the focus of the potent Dallas offense. In the second quarter, Dorsett got free on the near sidelines and started sprinting. A touchdown appeared inevitable because he had raced past the Redskins defenders and the only Washington player running after him with speed and purpose was Green.

However, Green was on the opposite side of the field and had to angle over to try to run down the speedy Dorsett. Simple high-school geometry showed that Green was running the hypotenuse length of the right triangle. Dorsett was running fast. But with each step they both took Green was eating up yardage. He took down Dorsett after a 77-yard run, and the Cowboys were forced to settle for a field goal.

That play would be the spur for a great rookie season. Green would start all 16 games and register 109 tackles and two inter-ceptions. He was a big part of a team that would storm through the regular season with a 14–2 record and then overwhelm the Los Angeles Rams in the divisional playoffs and survive a San Francisco 49ers comeback to win the NFC championship. The Redskins were significant favorites to beat the Los Angeles Raiders in Super Bowl XVIII in Tampa, Florida, but they got hammered, 38–9.

"We would come back and win a couple of Super Bowls and those are feelings that mean so much to me," Green said. "To play and become a champion in this sport is so satisfying. But that day we lost to the Raiders, it hurt and it hurt plenty. We expected to win and we had played so well all season. But they were more ready than we were and they took it away from us."

As Green's career progressed, he became a bigger part of the Redskins' defense. While he never lost his speed—he won four NFL fastest man competitions—he learned how to battle bigger receivers on their turf. He would not engage in hand fighting or trying to get in a jam to throw a man who may have been 40 pounds heavier off stride. Instead, he would often play the outside coverage technique that would give the opposing quarterback the belief that the receiver was open. Then when the ball was in the air, Green would swoop in and either knock the pass down or steal it away.

Green's talents were not lost on opposing cornerbacks. Former Eagles, Saints, and Raiders corner Eric Allen competed against Green for 14 years and got to know how Green did his job.

"He used his speed to be able to see the quarterback through the receiver," Allen said. "That gave him an advantage because if the pressure was getting there fast, and the quarterback was going to have to throw early, he could see that ball and break on it."

Despite his lack of size, Green played a very physical game. He knew how to jump on receivers who were running short routes over the middle and if they hit him with a double move he had the speed to catch up and make the play. He was especially strong at handling the screen pass because he was far too quick for offensive linemen who were trying to create a lane for the running back. He easily darted through them and brought the play to a standstill for little or no gain.

In Washington's championship season of 1987, Green was instrumental in the Redskins' playoff wins over the Chicago Bears and the Minnesota Vikings. Chicago still had an overpowering defense that season and few thought the Redskins stood a chance at coming into Soldier Field and coming away with the win. But with the scored tied 14–14 in the third quarter, Green returned a punt 52 yards for a touchdown—even though he was playing with a broken rib.

"I could really feel it about the last 30 yards of that run," Green recalled. "But you could see the end zone and see how the blocking had developed. I was not thinking about the pain. I was thinking about not getting hit and getting into the end zone."

The Redskins held on for a 21–17 win.

A week later, Green forced a key fumble in the NFC Championship Game against Minnesota's Darrin Nelson that helped cement Washington's 17–10 victory. From there, the Redskins easily defeated the Denver Broncos, 42–10, in Super Bowl XXII. "We were a confident group that day," Green said. "We had been beaten pretty good when we played the Raiders in the Super Bowl [after the 1983 season] and I think coach Gibbs had us prepared as well as any team could have been. They got off to a lead but we overwhelmed them in the second quarter. That was it and we won the title."

The Redskins would add another championship following the 1991 season, when they defeated the Buffalo Bills, 37–14, in Super Bowl XXVI. Green's career would become a hallmark for consistency as he played through the 2002 season and finished with 54 interceptions and won the respect of two decades' worth of NFL receivers for the way he played the game.

#34

KEN HOUSTON

Ken Houston got his start in professional football as a safety during the passing revolution that became the signature of the American Football League. Sid Gillman directed the charge as the head coach of the San Diego Chargers. Al Davis in Oakland followed suit and so did Weeb Ewbank in New York. Hank Stram did the same in Kansas City.

It became clear that if you were going to succeed in the AFL, it took quarterbacks like Joe Namath, Len Dawson, Daryle Lamonica, and John Hadl. It became equally clear that if you were going to stand up to an assault from one of those quarterbacks, you needed to have a defensive back with sensational athletic ability, intelligence, guts, and playmaking skills.

The Raiders had Willie Brown, the Chiefs had Johnny Robinson and the Houston Oilers had Kenny Houston. Houston was 6-foot-3, 198 pounds, and he had all the physical gifts to be a tremendous safety. He had a long stride to go with his speed and agility. Those skills made him ideal for pass defense yet he was strong enough to also be a devastating tackler.

He was selected to two AFL All-Star games and 10 Pro Bowls over a 12-year period from 1968 through 1979. He retired following the 1980 season, recognized as the premier strong safety of his era. In 1994, he was honored as a member of the NFL's 75th Anniversary Team. He intercepted 49 passes, which he returned for 898 yards. He also recovered 21 fumbles and scored 12 touchdowns, nine on interceptions and one each on a punt return, fumble return, and blocked-field-goal return.

He made an impression on the rest of the league early in his rookie season after being drafted out of tiny Prairie View A&M in the ninth round. In an early-season game against the New York Jets, he scored two touchdowns by returning a blocked field 71 yards and a Joe Namath interception 43 yards. Both plays were instrumental in allowing the Oilers to come away with a 28–28 tie. Houston was anything but a shy rookie, and showed he was not intimidated by playing against the league's glamour team in America's biggest city.

Ken Houston was a hidden gem in the AFL. He dominated with his ability to play from sideline to sideline and he enjoyed a remarkable season with the Oilers in 1971, when he had nine interceptions and returned four for touchdowns to lead the league in that department. He also forced two fumbles, recovered two fumbles, and returned one of them for a touchdown. The Oilers only won four games that season and Houston's interceptions played a key role in three of them.

Houston remained an industry secret until the Oilers traded him to the Washington Redskins in 1973 for five veterans. Once he arrived in Washington, Houston became a mainstay in the Redskins' "Over-the-Hill Gang" and he was immediately one of head coach George Allen's favorite players.

Allen was enamored with Houston's knowledge on the football field and the fact that he was almost always in the right position to make a play. Allen, who had learned the pro game as an assistant with the Bears under George Halas and who had built a dominant Los Angeles Rams team in the late 1960s, favored knowledgeable veterans over athletic rookies. Allen had a "win now" philosophy and his chances of competing in the NFC and taking his team into the playoffs were dependent on execution and not making mistakes.

Houston excelled at all aspects of the game for the Redskins—and he did not make mistakes. "You could see he was just an outstanding defensive back," Allen said in a 1983 interview. "Every step on the field he took was one with a purpose. That's why he was such a big part of what we were doing with the Redskins. When you get a player who can do exactly what his coaches are talking about, that's extremely valuable. It shows the other players what has to be done and it's a much more effective way than a coach using words. It's the best example for other veteran players who understand."

The 1973 Redskins were a team that was on the verge of exploding when Houston was traded there. He made perhaps the pivotal play in a season that would see them win 10 games and a spot in the NFC playoffs.

In a game on October 8, 1973, against the rival Dallas Cowboys, Washington was leading 14–7 with 16 seconds remaining. Dallas had the ball in a fourth-and-goal situation when Cowboys running back Walt Garrison grabbed a swing pass and headed toward the end zone. Houston hit Garrison squarely and stopped him in his tracks, inches shorts of the goal line. With that play Houston instantly became a household name in Washington as the Redskins held on for the win.

"That's the biggest tackle I've made in my life," Houston told the *Washington Post*. "I was looking for that play. They had been trying to hit that flare all night. Dallas quarterback Craig Morton made a pump and I came up. As strong as he (Garrison) is, I thought he should have scored, but I managed to keep him out."

That tackle was just one play, but it showed what Houston was all about. He was an instinctive defender against the pass, but he hit like a truck against the run and he never backed down. "I coached a lot of great players with the Bears, Rams, and Redskins," Allen said, "and Houston was as good as any of them. His knowledge and ability to turn that knowledge into a big play was just fantastic."

#35

RANDY MOSS

If Charles Barkley went a step too far when he said "I am not a role model," then Randy Moss seems to have expanded on that statement and turned it into a manifesto.

By the whole of Moss's career, it appears that he played when he wanted to play. But when he felt the urge to show what he could do on a football field, he was a one-man wrecking crew. He was capable of destroying the opposition merely by running down the field, sticking his hands up in the air, and then coming down with the ball while on his way to the endzone.

Moss's career can be divided into four phases that seem to indicate his level of interest:

Phase 1: He wanted to play in the first six years of his career with the Vikings, averaging 87.5 catches for 1,395.8 yards and 12.8 touchdowns per season.

Phase 2: He didn't want to play in his final season in Minnesota nor in the two years he was in Oakland, averaging only 50.3 catches for 775 yards and 8 touchdowns during those three seasons.

Phase 3: He wanted to play in his first three seasons in New England, averaging 83.3 catches for 1,255 yards and 15.7 touchdowns.

Phase 4: Moss had little left in the tank as he played for the Patriots, Titans, and Vikings in 2010, didn't play in 2011, and then attempted a comeback with the 49ers in 2012 that confirmed he was no longer a game-changing NFL player.

"When healthy, he's a definite force," said former Chargers head coach Marty Schottenheimer. "When he goes full speed, you know he's the target. When he doesn't, you know he's not in the play. When he's playing, you have to account for him. When I was coaching in San Diego, he wasn't much of a factor in the two years he played against us."

A six-time Pro Bowler and four-time first-team All-Pro selection, Moss was machine-like when he was being inspired. He put numbers on the board that exceeded those of any of his peers and could be challenged by only Jerry Rice. His career numbers left him second all-time in touchdown receptions (behind Rice and ahead of Terrell Owens), fourth in total touchdowns, and third in receiving yards per game.

As impressive as his numbers in the first and third phases are, the numbers in the second and fourth phases also tell a story, though. When Moss could hardly have cared about being on the football field and would have been much happier going fishing or smoking a joint—his words to *Sports Illustrated*—he still did a solid job by NFL standards. A receiver who can average those numbers would also have found himself on the receiving end of a three-year, $30 million contract.

The lack of production in the final phase tells another story as well. Most savvy veterans find a way to contribute at the end of their careers when they have lost a step and a few inches off of their vertical leap. The overall experience factor leaves the veteran with savvy and know-how that allows him to make key contributions at big moments. That's not how Moss finished his career.

Moss may not have had the classic makeup during the majority of his career, but he was undeniably productive on the football field. When he bought into the system, he was also a solid force in the locker room. After moving to New England in 2007 for the absurdly low price of a fourth-round draft pick, Moss was reborn. He knew he was with a team that had a good chance to win a championship and he played as if his life depended on it, making big plays all season and scoring an NFL-record 23 touchdowns. Moss may not have given much to the attending media, but he was supportive of his teammates and unafraid to show his commitment to them. When the Pats beat the Colts 24-20 in a Week 9 showdown between the NFL's unbeatens in Indianapolis, it was Moss who was in the locker room passing out hugs and high fives to his teammates, telling them how important they were to the team.

A year later, the Patriots suffered what could have been a death blow when quarterback Tom Brady went down with a season-ending knee injury in the first quarter of the first game of the season against the Kansas City Chiefs. Nevertheless, Moss spent hours in the film room working with backup Matt Cassel, getting to know his quarterback and helping his quarterback get to know him. The Patriots missed the playoffs in 2008, but they still finished with an 11-5 record, exceeding all expectations for a team that lost its future Hall of Fame quarterback.

Moss's effort to work with his new quarterback did not surprise Tennessee quarterback Kerry Collins, who had played with Moss during their time in Oakland. "Bringing Moss in was a great move by New England," Collins said. "The one thing that struck me when

I played with Randy in Oakland was just how much attention he gets on the field from defenses. His presence on the field helped the other receivers. When we played in Oakland, he was a little dinged up, but when he's full speed and at his best, he's by far the most gifted receiver I ever played with. His route running was better than I thought it would be, and his deep routes are a clinic."

Like Collins, there are others who defend Moss, saying injuries were a big factor during his two years in Oakland. However, even taking those injuries into account, Moss has shown plenty of disinterest on the field when he is not the focus of the play. Cameras have often focused on him leisurely jogging off the line and not even attempting to fool the defense by running a pass pattern.

Moss has never liked the idea of defending himself to the media. He says that his teammates have never had a problem with his effort and that's good enough for him. "I don't really like to answer questions like that because the people that question it probably never played football in their life or been on the same pedestal that I've been on," he told the *Boston Globe*. "I have a microscope [on me], and my microscope is very big.

"The people that talk about me as far as my work ethic and my competitive nature and me going out there and playing football, the best thing I can say is all you have to do is line up against me and see what happens. My coaches that I've played for, the players that I've played with, never seemed to have a problem about me and my character; only the media does."

But even with the imperfections, Moss has been the second-most dominant receiver the game has seen since the 1970 merger, and he came close to the great Jerry Rice on his best days. However, Rice never had those seemingly disinterested days, and that's why he has the edge on the ultra-talented Moss.

#36

ROGER STAUBACH

It took Roger Staubach nearly six years before he got an opportunity to play in the NFL following his Heisman Trophy-winning season at Navy in 1963. In the early and mid-1960s, the military academies would not even entertain the idea of giving an athlete a break from his military service commitment after graduation.

Staubach, of course, knew this and he never had a problem with it. He served his time, did his job, had a one-year tour of duty in Vietnam, and then joined the Dallas Cowboys in 1969. He was a godsend as far as Tom Landry was concerned. Landry had coached the Cowboys from their inception in 1960 and had gotten decent quarterback play from Don Meredith and Craig Morton. But

Meredith, a notorious night owl, was somewhat erratic and his training methods were unusual to say the least. Morton played with effort but everything was a struggle for him.

Imagine Landry's delight when Staubach came aboard. Landry was a trained engineer aside from his football career. Precision and discipline were his watchwords in running his team. It didn't take him more than a few practice sessions to realize that Staubach was cut from the same cloth and was as demanding of himself as any player he had ever coached.

In addition, Staubach's brilliant talent continued to shine through every time he took a snap. He had a strong and accurate arm, a quick release, saw the pass rush well and could get out of trouble and avoid mistakes. He split time with Morton his first two seasons, and the team projected a different aura depending on which quarterback was under center. With the slow-footed Morton, the Cowboys might get the occasional big play but the feeling was that it was just a matter of time before he would make a crucial mistake.

With the agile Staubach, the exact opposite feeling prevailed. Even though he made an occasional error, the mood was that he could overcome errors and mistakes and still get his team downfield to make a big play and lead the Cowboys to the win. This came to the fore in 1971. Staubach became the team's full-time quarterback and the Cowboys crossed over the line and won their first Super Bowl.

Staubach was brilliant that season, completing 126 of 211 passes for 1,882 yards with 15 touchdowns, four interceptions, and a 104.8 passer rating. He averaged 8.9 yards per pass and that remarkable figure got the Cowboys over the top. He won the Super Bowl MVP in the Cowboys' 24–3 win over the Miami Dolphins in Super Bowl VI. Three more passer-rating titles came his way, in addition to earning another championship ring with a win over the Denver Broncos in Super Bowl XII.

Staubach believes that his association with Landry was a great development for his career. "Coach Landry was so organized and always spent a lot of time on preparation," Staubach said. "And he had goals that were outstanding—reasonable goals, believable and achievable—and he measured them as a coach. And, I think that's why he had a 20-year winning streak. It was through preparation. I've really believed in business that you have to work hard and you have to be prepared and you have to develop a consistency, which he taught me as a coach. Plus, you have to do things right. He was a person—you read about him but he's even better than that. He taught me a lot about walking your talk and living your life and doing the right thing. And he knew the game of football and he had us well-prepared."

While the historical picture between Staubach and Landry is a beautiful one, the actual co-existence between the two was not all sweetness and light. Staubach was a scrambler like Minnesota's Fran Tarkenton and that irked Landry from time to time. On the other hand, Landry's play calling almost invariably had the Cowboys start their games with a predictable ground game and they wouldn't start throwing the ball until later on. Staubach tried to influence Landry to open up sooner, but it was a difficult argument to win.

"He had to put up with my scrambling, but I had to put up with his play calling," said Staubach. Eventually there was a meeting of the minds, but like most compromises, neither Landry nor Staubach were left completely happy. But that did not stop the two from forging a great partnership. Staubach's ability to run with the ball may have gotten under Landry's skin on occasion, but that ability changed the way the game was scouted and executed. While Tarkenton may have been the forerunner of running quarterbacks, Staubach refined that way of playing. He scrambled to step out of trouble, buy time and make plays on the run. He ran the ball as a last resort. Shortly thereafter, the concept of having a mobile quarterback was universally accepted. Teams no longer wanted a "pocket passer" at quarterback. Most wanted a quarterback who could make plays on the run. There have been notable exceptions like Dan Marino and Peyton

Manning, but almost all the great quarterbacks since the Staubach era have had some degree of mobility.

"I couldn't have asked for more from a quarterback than I got from Roger," Landry said prior to Denver's Super Bowl XXXII win over the Green Bay Packers. "He was all about leadership and clutch performances. When he was on the field everyone knew that we had a chance to win."

Staubach's leadership qualities may have been as important as his arm strength, quick release, and ability to read defenses. "Roger always believed that when he took the field the Cowboys had a chance to win," said former Cowboys tight end Billy Joe Dupree. "It didn't matter if we were down by two touchdowns or more. He was confident and he always believed we could do it. Some guys just talk it; Roger actually believed it and we believed in him."

FRAN TARKENTON VS. ROGER STAUBACH								
	Att	Comp	Yards	TD	Int	Rush Yds	Rush TD	W-L-T
Fran Tarkenton	6,467	3,686	47,003	342	266	3,674	32	124-109-6
Roger Staubach	2,958	1,685	22,700	153	109	2,264	20	85-29-0

#37

JUNIOR SEAU

Junior Seau, like Dick Butkus, was a great player on a bad team for the majority of his career. Seau's San Diego Chargers had their moments, none better than the 1994 season when they won the AFC before being totally overmatched in the Super Bowl by the 49ers. But most of the time they weren't very competitive. They could not climb over the .500 mark in 10 of Seau's 13 seasons for his hometown team.

As a result, there was an undercurrent of whispers hinting that Seau had been overrated. Even though he had been a Pro Bowl player in all but his rookie season and had been a first-team All-Pro six times, Seau's image started to get the best of his onfield production.

Talk about a mistaken impression. Seau went on to play parts of three seasons with the Dolphins and three more with the Patriots. Injuries held him back from time-to-time in those six years, but when he was in the lineup he was still a dominant player who could run, diagnose the play, and make the tackle.

Seau had retired after the 2007 season, but when the Patriots were hit by injuries in second half of the 2008 season, Bill Belichick called Seau and asked him to return to help the Pats finish the season. "I had kept myself in shape and I had wanted to play all along," Seau said. "When I got the call from Bill and he said he needed me, that's what I needed to hear. A football player has to be needed to be able to play. That's all I needed to hear."

Seau was needed by his team for all of the 13 years he was in San Diego. Throughout most of that time, the Chargers could not do much on the offensive side of the ball. But even in the worst of the Chargers' seasons, Seau simply refused to allow opponents to run the football. In 2000, the Chargers were an atrocious 1-15 and had the worst offense in the league. Opponents had little trouble throwing the ball on them, but even with all their difficulties, San Diego allowed only 3.0 yards per carry, second only to the formidable Ravens defense which gave up 2.7 yards per attempt.

Skeptics might point out that the offense gave away so many turnovers and the defense was quite vulnerable against the pass, so the run defense figures were skewed. Actually, that's not true. The Chargers were behind most of the time and usually by a lot in the second half of games. It's at that point when teams want to run to keep the clock moving and get the game over with. So the Chargers were playing phenomenal run defense and much of it was Seau's doing.

He always took special pride in stopping the run, whether it was in San Diego, Miami, or New England. "They wanted to run the ball on us and put their imprint on the game and their footprints on us," Seau explained. "That could not be allowed to happen. I viewed it as my job to stop the run and they were trying to show they had more talent, ability and desire. That was not a battle that I was going to let someone else win."

It was precisely that attitude that made Seau a wanted commodity in Miami and New England in the latter part of his career. Many questioned Belichick when he brought in the 37-year-old Seau prior to the 2006 season, but the move paid off because the Pats went from the 17th ranked defensive team in the league to the 2nd. Seau, who continued to show the ability to go from sideline-to-sideline to make plays, had 69 tackles (30 solo) and played a key role in the leadership of the defense.

Seau's best season probably took place in the Chargers' Super Bowl season of 1994, when he posted 155 tackles (124 solo), 5.5 sacks, and 3 fumble recoveries. He was the focus of a 49er offense that took the field knowing it was the superior team. "We were very confident entering that game," said 49er tight end Brent Jones. "We had Steve Young, Jerry Rice, Ricky Watters and we felt we couldn't be stopped," Jones said. "But at the same time they had Junior Seau. We knew he was a great player and we had to respect him. We ran most of our plays in areas where he was not going to be a factor. We didn't want to take any risks by putting the ball in his area any more than we had to."

Jones was talking about Seau's relentlessness. The 49ers knew that Seau was capable of destroying a running game and wreaking havoc all by himself. He maintained that level of play throughout his run in San Diego and he recovered at the end of his career to demonstrate that ability with the Patriots. When Belichick decided to pick up the phone, he called Seau even though he was nearing the end of his first season of retirement.

Seau would finish his career in 2009, and he appeared to settle comfortably into retirement with several media jobs. However, Seau's life ended tragically when he committed suicide in 2012. Seau's family sued the NFL in 2013 over brain injuries he suffered during the course of his career.

#38

ERIC DICKERSON

There are great athletes who combine talent, hard work and team play and find a way into the hearts of the American sports fan. Then there are athletes who have talent and ability, care little about team play, and still find a way to dominate.

The latter description sums up Eric Dickerson in a nutshell. Dickerson broke the NFL record for rushing yards in a season in his second year and appeared to be an unstoppable force. However, despite posting 11,226 rushing yards over his first seven NFL seasons, holdouts, perceived slights, and frequent moves kept him from becoming the player he might have been.

Nobody was more impressed with Dickerson's talent than the late Walter Payton, who held the NFL rushing record until Emmitt Smith passed him. Payton loved watching Dickerson's ultra-smooth running style and thought that when Dickerson was with the Rams, he had a chance to take the all-time rushing record, stuff it in his back pocket and take it out past the 20,000-yard mark.

Dickerson was a dominant running back but the underlying theme when one looks at his career is that he could have done so much more. However, what he did do was quite impressive and made him a worthy Hall of Fame enshrinee in 1999.

Go back to his rookie season in 1983. That was the year of the great quarterback draft class that included John Elway and Dan Marino, but Dickerson was the class's top running back. The record-setting back out of Southern Methodist University was selected with the second overall pick by the Los Angeles Rams.

Dickerson was as nervous as he could be at the start of his rookie campaign, fumbling six times in the first few weeks of the season. However, he turned the corner with an 85-yard TD run against the Jets and the yards and touchdowns started piling up after that. Dickerson finished his rookie season with 1,808 yards (a record for rookies) on 390 carries. He posted 18 rushing touchdowns (also a record for rookies) and added 51 receptions out of the backfield.

Considering how shaky Dickerson was at the start of the season it was an amazing performance. "I was so nervous in my first few games," Dickerson said. "Especially that first game. When I put my helmet on I could not remember a thing about the play that was called, what I was supposed to do or anything. I could barely remember to breathe."

Even if he was nervous, Dickerson still gained 255 yards in his first three games. However, his breakout performance against the Jets served notice regarding what kind of back he would be in the NFL. He rushed for 192 yards and two touchdowns in the game, including the aforementioned 85-yarder that showed his remarkable speed with the ball in his hands.

It also showed off Dickerson's unique running style. Dickerson defied convention and NFL logic by running the ball with a straight-up stance. Instead of crouching and making himself low as he prepared to cut, Dickerson would run fully erect and seemingly leave himself as a target for marauding linebackers and defensive backs.

Head coach John Robinson was clearly worried about Dickerson, but the running back had no concerns at all about taking hellacious shots. "I run upright mostly when I see daylight, so if you watch film you'll see I don't get hit in the chest much," Dickerson said. "They can't hit what they can't catch."

Dickerson's analysis was fairly accurate. He almost never got hit with the full-out shots that other backs absorbed. He had the ability to accelerate when he sensed contact was about to come. "I knew when I was about to get hit," Dickerson said. "I would try to turn it up another notch or make a move. I did not want to get hit and I was pretty good at making them miss."

After his brilliant rookie season, Dickerson went on to have the most prolific year any running back has ever had. His 2,105 yards in 1984 is a record that still stands 25 years later and included four games of 175 rushing yards or more and 12 games rushing for 100 yards. He bested O. J. Simpson's single-season record by 102 yards and Dickerson appeared to be in a position to make his mark on all the NFL rushing records.

But after the glory, Dickerson looked to cash in and he engaged the Rams in a long holdout that lasted through the third game of the 1985 season. Two years later, he pushed the Rams into a trade that landed him in Indianapolis.

Dickerson had averaged 1,750 yards in his first four seasons with the Rams. He would hit the 1,659-yard mark in his first full season with the Colts, but that would be his last phenomenal season. Dickerson had complaints about the way he was used in Indianapolis and the coaching staff; after four seasons in Indianapolis he was traded to the Raiders in 1992. After a year with the silver and black, he was traded to the Atlanta Falcons, with whom he played just four lackluster games before calling it a career.

He ended his 11-year career with 13,259 rushing yards a 4.4 yards-per-carry mark, and 96 total touchdowns. He is clearly one of the most talented and most effective backs that ever played, but he also left the game with the feeling that Payton was right and that he could have been even more spectacular than he was.

BEST FIRST EIGHT YEARS RUSHING

Player	Att	Yards	Avg	Rush TD
Eric Dickerson	2,616	11,903	4.6	86
LaDainian Tomlinson	2,657	11,760	4.4	126
Barry Sanders	2,384	11,725	4.9	84
Emmitt Smith	2,595	11,234	4.3	112
Jim Brown	2,070	10,768	5.2	89
Walter Payton	2,352	10,204	4.3	72
Adrian Peterson*	2,033	10,115	5	86
Thurman Thomas	2,285	9,729	4.3	48
O.J. Simpson	1,997	9,626	4.8	57
Tony Dorsett	2,136	9,525	4.5	59
Marshall Faulk	2,155	9,442	4.4	79
Earl Campbell	2,187	9,407	4.3	74

*--First seven years; Peterson entering eighth season in 2014

#39

CHUCK BEDNARIK

In a sport dominated by fearless warriors, Chuck Bednarik is in the team picture of the toughest guys to ever play the game . . . not only in the picture, but in the front row.

Dick Butkus, Deacon Jones, Big Daddy Lipscomb, Joe Greene, Jack Lambert, Doug Atkins, Gino Marchetti, Randy White, Dan Hampton, Lawrence Taylor, Charles Haley, Ray Lewis, and Jack Youngblood make my list. Whether others should be included is open to great debate, but put all of those players mentioned in a room and let them have at it. The guess here is that Bednarik, Butkus, or Taylor would emerge.

Jim Brown, perhaps the greatest football player of all time, is a man of immense pride. When Brown issues a compliment to another athlete, it's worth noting. "Chuck Bednarik was as great as any linebacker who has ever lived," Brown said. "I don't know how old he is, but I'll bet nobody could kick his butt today."

Bednarik was born in 1925. He was 79 when Brown made his assessment.

Bednarik played center on offense and middle linebacker on defense for the Philadelphia Eagles. He was the last of the two-way players. He was called the "60-minute man," but that was a bit of an exaggeration. Bednarik played every snap on offense and every snap on defense, but he was on the sidelines for kickoffs. In the 1960 NFL Championship Game, he was on the field for more than 58 actual game minutes.

He is best known for two legendary plays: a knockout hit on Frank Gifford in the Eagles' 1960 championship season and a last-second tackle of Jim Taylor that preserved Philadelphia's win over the Green Bay Packers in that season's title game.

The Gifford hit has reverberated around the NFL for decades. With the Eagles leading the Giants 17-10 in the fourth quarter of their 1960 battle for first place in the Eastern Conference at Yankee Stadium, New York had the ball and was driving for a possible tying touchdown. Giants quarterback George Shaw hit Gifford with a pass over the middle and before he could make a move upfield, he was met head-on by Bednarik.

The full-speed hit sent Gifford flying backwards, his head hitting the frozen turf and his arms and legs splaying backwards. The football rolled away and Gifford did not move. The great stadium went silent after hearing the hit and seeing the results. Eagles linebacker Chuck Weber fell on the ball and recovered. A *Sports Illustrated* photo seemed to indicate Bednarik was celebrating the damage he had done to Gifford, but he was merely reacting to his team's recovery of the ball and the fact that it ensured victory.

"I said, 'This game is over,'" Bednarik recalled. "I wasn't directing it at Frank. I was just happy we won. If people think I was gloating over Frank, they couldn't have been more wrong."

Nevertheless, that play symbolized what Bednarik was all about and the standard that he set. The Eagles went on to win the Eastern Conference title, earning the right to meet the up-and-coming Packers and Vince Lombardi for the league championship.

Even though the game was played in Philadelphia, most experts expected the Packers to win. Green Bay had Bart Starr, Paul Hornung, Jim Taylor, Willie Davis, and, of course, Vince Lombardi prowling the sidelines.

The Eagles had an aging Bednarik, Norm Van Brocklin playing in what turned out to be the last game of his career, and a slew of role players. The Eagles played with passion and guts and held a 17–13 lead in the closing seconds. However, Green Bay held the ball at the Philadelphia 22-yard line with time for one last play.

Starr could not find an open receiver in the end zone, so he dumped the ball off to Taylor, a concrete block of a man who lowered his head and powered his way to the 9-yard line.

Bednarik was right there to meet him. He stopped Taylor, got him to the ground, and would not get off of him until the game was over.

"Taylor was moving and squirming, trying to get up," Bednarik recalled. "But there was no way I was getting up and letting them have another play. Taylor cursed at me and told me to get off of him and I did just that [when] the second hand hit zero. It was a great win and a great achievement because we did not have a lot of talent. I don't know how we did it, but we won the game."

Bednarik was not just on the delivering end when it came to pain. During his 14-year career, he missed only three games and two of those were as rookie. The force of his hitting took a toll on his own body. In particular, his hands now look like something out of a movie because none of his fingers extend straight out. They have all been bent, gnarled, and misshapen.

Chuck Bednarik

During a preseason game toward the end of his career, Bednarik played off a block, made a hit on a runner, and felt a searing pain in his arm. He had torn his biceps muscle and it slipped from his upper arm to his forearm.

"Chuck pushed the muscle back in its place and went to the sidelines," Eagles' teammate Tom Brookshier said. "He told the doctor to put some tape around it and he went back in. It was an *exhibition* game and he was playing like it was for the championship. That's the way he played all the time and that's why he became the great player he was."

Bednarik recognizes that today's athletes are bigger and stronger than they were during his career. But the differences in size and athleticism are not enough to make a difference as to whether at 6-foot-3, 235-pound linebacker could still have the same impact. "A reporter once asked me if I thought I could play with the guys playing today," Bednarik said. "I told him his question was an insult. Of course I could play today. And I would be a star."

Period. End of story.

#40

THURMAN THOMAS

The picture has become one of the NFL rites of passage on Draft Day. Every year as the draft moves through its first round, the cameras focus on the Green Room. That's where many of the top prospects in the draft sit, waiting to be trotted out to shake hands with the commissioner and don the hat of the team that drafts them.

While there are a lot of smiling faces among the players who are called at the top of the draft, there is a painful awkwardness for the final players in the Green Room who get called. Everyone realizes that money is slipping away as anticipation turns into disappointment.

The first player who had to endure this live in front of ESPN cameras in the Green Room was Thurman Thomas in 1988. He was finally drafted by the Buffalo Bills with the 40th overall pick—well into the second round. Thomas had been a brilliant runner at Oklahoma State, and most of the scouting reports indicated that he had what it took to be an NFL star. But what he also had was a damaged knee. The reports said that Thomas was playing on a knee that was "bone on bone," and surgery would not be an option if he suffered another knee injury because there was no more cartilage or ligament to repair. His career would be over. As a result, Thomas dropped like a stone until Buffalo Bills general manager Bill Polian and head coach Marv Levy took a chance on him.

To say that Thomas came into the NFL with a chip on his shoulder is like saying that George W. Bush had just a bit of a problem with the economy. Thomas was a motivated performer. He wanted to show everyone in the league who had bypassed him that they had made a big mistake. His entire career was based on that premise.

He succeeded in his goal. Thomas became one of the best running backs of his time and one of the most productive backs of all-time. The 1991 league MVP, Thomas led the NFL in total yards from scrimmage four consecutive years (1989–1992) and became one of only four running backs to rush for 1,000 yards or more in eight straight seasons. As of the writing of this book, his 12,074 rushing yards ranks him 12th all-time in league annals.

Thomas played on all four of the Bills' Super Bowl teams, and of course, he tasted defeat four times. However, he put on a performance for the ages in Super Bowl XXV against the Giants when he rushed for 135 yards and caught five passes for 55 yards. That Super Bowl slipped away from the Bills when Scott Norwood's field goal attempt sailed wide right, but his running had Giants head coach Bill Parcells and linebacker Lawrence Taylor feeling the pressure. "He was on our minds throughout the game," Taylor said. "He was as difficult for us to contain and keep track of as any running back we ever faced."

While Thomas did not play as well in his other Super Bowls and committed a memorable gaffe in Super Bowl XXVI against the Washington Redskins when he could not find his helmet on the sidelines and was forced to miss the start of the game, he still earned entrance into the Hall of Fame and is remembered as one of the most versatile backs of in NFL history.

Thomas specialized in getting the job done with his quickness and smooth moves. He could hit full speed in an instant and then fake defenders completely out of position with a head fake or even just a look to the outside. His ability to cut quickly had defenders playing on their heels throughout the game.

Thomas may have been at his best in 1991 and 1992, when he led the league in total yards from scrimmage both seasons. Thomas rushed for 1,407 yards and averaged 4.9 yards per attempt in 1991 while catching 62 passes for 631 yards. A year later, Thomas rushed for 1,487 yards and caught 58 passes for 626 yards. Thomas was not the kind of player who would call attention to himself in the locker room, but he became one of the Bills' team leaders because of his production.

"Thurman wasn't the guy in the locker room who would stand up and say a lot, but when he got on the football field that's when his leadership came out," said Bills quarterback Jim Kelly. "Things he would say to offensive linemen on the sidelines and things he would say in the huddle. He'd say things on the field that would keep us going. Behind the scenes the attitude he brought to the game once he was on the football field was something not many people had a chance to see."

Levy was impressed with the business-like attitude and the professionalism Thomas brought to the field. "He was the most consistent player we had," Levy said. "You could always count on Thurman for his effort and his production because he was so determined. Underneath it all was the fire that started, I believe, when he was drafted. It was disappointing for him but it was a great day for the Buffalo Bills. He took out his frustration on his opponents and that's why he got to the Hall of Fame."

#41

BART STARR

Bart Starr is perhaps the most underrated performer in NFL history. People who aren't old enough to have seen him play see his statistics and see that the most passes he ever threw in a season was 295 and that 16 touchdown passes was the most he ever threw in a year. Ordinary numbers for an ordinary quarterback.

Nothing could be further from the truth. First off, Starr won five NFL championships in a seven-year period, including three in a row. Joe Montana won four titles and so did Terry Bradshaw. Nobody ever won more from 1960 going forward.

Take a look inside the numbers. Starr may be more responsible for turning the NFL into a passing league than any other individual. Here's why:

The Green Bay Packers had a redoubtable ground attack with Jim Taylor and Paul Hornung. Later on, Chuck Mercein took on a key role as did Donny Anderson and Jim Grabowski. With Vince Lombardi at the helm, the Packers were seen as a running team. But the numbers disagree with the perception.

The Packers averaged 3.4 yards per carry in 1965, 11th-best in the NFL. However, their 8.2 yards per pass average ranked second in the league, and they defeated Jim Brown and the Cleveland Browns in the NFL Championship Game.

The Packers averaged 3.5 yards per rush in 1966, ranking 14th in the league, but they finished first in the league in yards per pass at 8.9 yards per attempt and they went on to beat the Dallas Cowboys in the NFL Championship Game.

In 1967, the Packers finished fourth in yards per rushing attempt at 4.0 per carry, a big improvement over the previous two seasons. But, once again, they finished first in the league with an average of 8.3 yards per pass. Starr averaged 8.7 yards per pass. (The team's figure is lower because he gave way in a couple of games to backup Zeke Bratkowski.) The Packers went on to beat the Dallas Cowboys in the "Ice Bowl" for the NFL championship and then beat the Oakland Raiders in Super Bowl II.

Starr averaged 7.8 yards per attempt for his career, a better figure than Dan Marino, Joe Montana, Peyton Manning, or Terry Bradshaw. He was accurate in every big game he played and he led the Packers to a 9–1 mark in postseason games, earning the MVP award in each of the first two Super Bowls.

He also came up with his most memorable performance under the horrific conditions of the Ice Bowl. The brutally cold game should have been a two-yards-and-a-cloud-of-dust taffy pull, but neither Starr nor underrated Dallas Cowboy quarterback Don Meredith would let that happen. The game came down to a last-minute drive that Starr directed with the temperature having dropped to minus-18 degrees. The drive is best remembered for Starr sneaking into the end zone over guard Jerry Kramer, whose block of Jethro Pugh was the decisive play in the game. However, while Starr ended the game with a run, he directed the drive by going 5 of 5 for 59 yards and defining the word leadership.

His memory of that final play is still as strong as ever.

"The play call was that Chuck Mercein would get the ball," Starr told Kerry Byrne of the website Cold, Hard, Football Facts. "That was our lead play in the game in that situation. We had recognized that the Cowboys had a very strong solid approach on short yardage. I don't know what they called it, but we labeled it the submarine technique. Their defensive linemen submarined down so well that you couldn't knock them back. But [Cowboys defensive tackle] Jethro Pugh was so tall, he couldn't get down as low as the other guys. So we thought we could get under him. We had run that play two other times in the game and got a minimum of two yards each time, so we knew it would work. But at the end of the game, the ground had grown so hard and a running play was a risk because of the ice on the ground.

"So I asked the linemen if they could get their footing for one play, and then on the sideline I said to coach that there's nothing wrong with the play. I said I can shuffle my feet and slide in. I felt like I was under control and not slipping. All he said to me was, 'Let's run it and get the hell out of here.'"

That championship, the Packers' third straight, is Starr's fondest memory of his football career.

Starr's career could very easily have never started. He was drafted out of Alabama in the 17th round of the 1956 draft. He was thought to have ordinary athletic ability and an ordinary arm. When Lombardi was hired by the Packers prior to the 1959 season, he spent much of the offseason looking at Packers films and he discovered that Starr had everything he was looking for in a quarterback. He was an accurate passer and had adequate arm strength. He had good mechanics, great ball-handling skills, read defenses well, and made excellent decisions.

Lombardi's assessment of what had been a non-descript first three years in the NFL for Starr was the key move behind Green Bay's championship run.

If the coach saw Starr as the ideal quarterback to lead his team, the quarterback saw Lombardi in similar terms. He didn't have any negatives from his perspective. "The man was so fundamentally strong and committed his life to the right priorities," Starr said. "It was God, family, and then the others—and we were the others. He wanted us to live our lives that way, too. It was a joy to work with him. He was very, very bright, extremely committed and uniquely well organized.

"Until he came, I was just one of the QBs there. We were being rotated and moved around. We had a come-from-behind win and from then on I was the starting QB. I think for him it was matter of him finding out who was going to be a leader. I can't say what he might have seen. But I was highly motivated to want to continue to improve and get an opportunity to show him. He gave us an opportunity and we were able to capitalize on it. I feel very fortunate to have him come along. He was everything I would have hoped for. A marvelous, marvelous teacher, coach, and leader. So when you have someone like that, it's very inspiring."

It's probably the best quarterback-coach combination in NFL history, with Bill Walsh and Joe Montana being a close second.

BART STARR'S CHAMPIONSHIP YEARS WITH THE GREEN BAY PACKERS										
YEAR	G	ATT	COMP	COMP %	YDS	Y/A	TD	INT	QB RATING	RESULT	OPPONENT
1961	14	295	172	58.3	2,418	8.2	16	16	80.3	Won NFL championship game	NYG
1962	14	285	178	62.5	2,483	8.6	12	9	90.7	Won NFL championship game	NYG
1965	14	251	140	55.8	2,055	8.2	16	9	89.0	Won NFL championship game	CLE
1966	14	251	156	62.2	2,257	9	14	3	105.0	Won Super Bowl	KC
1967	14	210	115	54.8	1,823	8.7	9	17	64.4	Won Super Bowl	OAK

#42

GENE UPSHAW

In the end, Gene Upshaw will be most remembered for his leadership of the NFL Players Association. Perhaps that's the way it should be, since he represented thousands of players as president of the union, a disorganized group that he took over in the late 1980s after the rudderless leadership of a lawyer named Ed Garvey, and turned into a powerful group that increased players' salary and benefits dramatically. His leadership was not without criticism, though, particularly from retired players who claimed he did not do enough for them.

But long before Upshaw's controversial career as a union leader and negotiator, he had unprecedented success on the football field as an offensive guard for the Oakland Raiders. At the time he was drafted from Texas A&I University with the 17th overall pick of the

1967 NFL Draft, Raiders owner Al Davis needed a guard who could block Kansas City Chiefs defensive tackle Buck Buchanan, one of the most destructive defensive linemen in the league. The Raiders had nobody who could fit that bill and Davis saw Upshaw as a big man (6-foot-5, 255 pounds) who had the speed, quickness, and blocking ability to deal with the explosive Buchanan. He was right.

"Gene was a great matchup for Buck," said Buchanan's Chiefs teammate, Tom Condon, who later served as Upshaw's (and many star players') agent. "It was very rare for a big man to get out and run like he did. The Raiders would run that weak-side lead, led by Art Shell and Gene Upshaw. And they'd continue to run because we couldn't stop it."

Upshaw became a dominant guard in the AFL. When that league merged with the NFL and the two leagues started playing an integrated schedule in 1970, Upshaw proved himself to be the best guard in football. He excelled as a run blocker, leading the Raiders sweep with backs Mark van Eeghen and Clarence Davis carrying the load and giving quarterbacks Daryle Lamonica and Ken Stabler adequate time to pass in the Raiders' downfield passing game. Before Upshaw had been drafted by the Raiders, they were a good team that couldn't quite get to the playoffs, finishing with 8–5–1 records in 1965 and '66. But in Upshaw's first season with the Raiders, they went 13–1 and put on a dominating performance in the AFL Championship Game against the Houston Oilers before losing Super Bowl II to Vince Lombardi's Green Bay Packers.

Upshaw held the left guard spot in the Raider lineup for 15 seasons, starting 207 straight regular-season games (second all-time among offensive lineman only to teammate Jim Otto's 210) until finally being forced out of action for one game in 1981. Upshaw returned the next week to play 10 more games in what turned out to be his final season. Honors came frequently for Upshaw. He was named first- or second-team All-League or All-Conference 11 consecutive years, and he was named to play in seven Pro Bowls. Upshaw was an intense, intelligent, dedicated competitor who used his excellent size and speed to his best advantage.

The Raiders were a dominant team in the Upshaw era, making the playoffs in 10 of his first 11 seasons and winning nine division titles. The team's signature season came in 1976, when they finished with a 13–1 record, beat the New England Patriots in the divisional playoffs and then the Steelers in the AFC title game. After overcoming Pittsburgh, a team that had eliminated the Raiders from the postseason in three of their four previous playoff meetings, they were giddy at the prospect of facing the Minnesota Vikings in the Super Bowl.

The key, as Raiders head coach John Madden saw it, would be how well the Raiders' outstanding blocking duo of Gene Upshaw and tackle Art Shell handled Vikings defensive tackle Alan Page and defensive end Jim Marshall. While Page and Marshall were two of the best defensive linemen in the NFL, the Raiders felt they had the edge in that matchup. "We knew how good Page and Marshall were, but we felt like our guys could handle that matchup pretty well," Madden said. "Gene was one of those guys who could do everything, pass protection as well as run-blocking. Very few guys are good in the trenches and out on the perimeter. Versatility, that's what he had throughout his career."

Neither Page nor Marshall registered a mark on the stat-sheet that day. Between the two of them, neither man had a tackle, a sack, a pass deflection, or a forced fumble. It was complete domination by the Raiders' offensive line and the result was a 32–13 victory that was even more one-sided than the final score would indicate. After the game, the beleaguered Page could only admit the obvious: "We got whipped," he said glumly.

It was an explanation that many Raiders opponents would echo over the years, particularly defensive linemen who had to try to get past Upshaw. He continued to be effective when he moved from the trenches to the boardroom, taking the NFLPA from a union that had been defeated at every turn in its dealings with the league to one that was near-equal partners. It's quite a legacy.

#43

LANCE ALWORTH

The phrase is "yards after catch." Nearly every football fan knows it and those that participate in fantasy football are especially interested in it. The yards a receiver gains after catching the ball is a key factor in distinguishing good receivers from average ones and great ones from good ones.

Lance Alworth excelled in that area before the phrase was even coined. Alworth may have been the American Football League's first great star. He was certainly in the right place at the right time as he combined with quarterback John Hadl and a brilliant strategist in head coach Sid Gillman to give the San Diego Chargers the AFL's premier pitch-and-catch combination. There was little recognition for Alworth, Hadl, and other AFL stars at the time, because they were competing with the NFL and their achievements were pooh-poohed, dismissed and treated as if they were the older league's poor relations. But the AFL players knew better. They knew better because many of them had been high draft picks in the NFL and few had been pursued harder than Alworth was.

Alworth was drafted eighth overall in the 1962 NFL draft by the San Francisco 49ers. The AFL's Oakland Raiders had drafted Alworth with the ninth spot in their draft and quickly traded his rights to the Chargers, who were a more complete team at the time and wanted a game-breaking wide receiver to give them a championship edge. San Francisco head coach Red Hickey tried to persuade Alworth to sign with his the 49ers, but he was up against Chargers assistant coach and chief recruiter Al Davis, the same Al Davis who would go on to own the Raiders. At that time, he was learning football from Gillman, a man whose innovative mind and strategic planning gave him a significant edge on the competition.

A battle between Davis and Hickey proved to be no contest. Davis sold Alworth on what the Chargers were trying to do with their offense—attack downfield through the air—and why the AFL was the place to be. The Chargers promised Alworth a no-cut contract. When Alworth informed Hickey that the Chargers had offered him such a deal, Hickey decided to match it. But Alworth knew that the 49ers were looking at him as just a piece of their business and he didn't feel like he was truly wanted—it left a bad tasted in his mouth. Davis also promised Alworth he would play right away.

That didn't happen, though, because Alworth suffered a freak injury in his first training camp while kicking a football. He tore a muscle in his right leg and played just four games before the end of the year, catching 10 passes and scoring three touchdowns. His numbers were remarkable after that. In the next six years, Alworth caught 384 passes for 7,747 yards and 70 touchdowns, averaging 20.2 yards every time he caught the ball. By comparison, Jerry Rice averaged 15.4 yards per reception during his career and averaged better than 20 yards per catch only once in his 20-year career.

Alworth did not have Joe Montana or Steve Young throwing him the ball, either. At the start he had an aging veteran in Tobin Rote before the strong-armed but raw Hadl arrived on the scene. Through the 1964 season, Alworth got open using his 9.6 speed (he ran the 100-yard dash as well as the 220 as a track star at the University of Arkansas). After that, however, the word was out in the AFL: in order to have a chance to cover Alworth—known by his nickname of "Bambi" for his large brown eyes and for the way he ran—you had to double-cover him. The decision forced Alworth to build up a series of moves he could use to always get him open.

Alworth learned how to make his moves by watching films of Houston Oilers wide receiver Charlie Hennigan. He saw that Hennigan ran every pattern with a purpose, whether he was getting passes thrown his way or not. "I saw that every step he made had a purpose," Alworth explained. "When I ran a square out, it was kind of a circle. Charlie ran these crisp routes and every step counted for something. I saw there was a lot I could do to improve [my technique]."

While Alworth improved his route-running, that was never the focus of his game and Gillman never expected it to be. He wanted Alworth to get to a certain point on the field and then break off his route when Hadl expected him to make his move. The two had expert timing and the quarterback and coach always expected Alworth to come away with the ball even if it was thrown into a crowd. That was because the 6-foot-2 Alworth had superb leaping ability—at least as far as catching a football was concerned. "I played a lot of basketball when I was young and when I tried to cram it [dunk] after practice I couldn't," Alworth explained. "But in a game there were pictures of me going above the rim to get a rebound. The same was true in football. I could go over the linebackers and defensive backs and get it."

That's when Alworth's run–after–the–catch ability took hold. He came down ready to run and didn't need to gather himself after making a spectacular catch. His feet would hit the ground running, and the defense rarely caught him.

Alworth also took to blocking like few other wide receivers did. Gillman demanded it of him and all the Chargers receivers, but Alworth found that it was an area that benefited him as a receiver. "If I block for Paul Lowe and the running game, it makes me a more dangerous receiver," Alworth told *Sports Illustrated*. "If I make a block that gets him into the open field, he's going to want to do the same for me. And that's just how it has worked."

In 1978, Alworth became the first AFL player inducted into the Pro Football Hall of Fame. He was an All–AFL performer seven times led the league in receiving yards and receptions three times. He still holds the Chargers franchise records for receiving touchdowns (83) and receiving yards (9,584).

Run after the catch—the term was invented for Alworth.

SAN DIEGO CHARGERS ALL-TIME RECEIVING LEADERS

Player	Years	G	Rec	Yds	Y/R	TD
1. Lance Alworth	1962-1970	110	493	9584	19.4	81
2. Charlie Joiner	1976-1986	164	586	9203	15.7	47
3. Antonio Gates	2003-2013	163	719	9193	12.8	87
4. Gary Garrison	1966-1976	131	404	7533	18.6	58
5. Kellen Winslow	1979-1987	109	541	6741	12.5	45
6. Wes Chandler	1981-1987	94	373	6132	16.4	41
7. Anthony Miller	1988-1993	93	374	5582	14.9	37
8. Tony Martin	1994-1997	64	288	4184	14.5	33
9. LaDainian Tomlinson	2001-2009	141	530	3955	7.5	15
10. Ronnie Harmon	1990-1995	96	378	3939	10.4	12

#44

JACK LAMBERT

There is little doubt that Jack Lambert was one of the toughest and meanest players to ever play in the NFL. He was a dominant athlete who took over the leadership role for the Pittsburgh Steelers in 1976 when Joe Greene started to feel the impact of nagging injuries. Lambert, big, mean, and raw in his No. 58 jersey, channeled Dick Butkus as he went sideline to sideline to punish ball carriers. But what makes Lambert's outstanding, Hall of Fame career so shocking is that when he came into the league as a second-round pick from Kent State in 1974, he weighed only 204 pounds.

While he stood an imposing 6-foot-4, Lambert was downright skinny. But despite his weight disadvantage there have been few players as intimidating as Lambert. He was a remarkable athlete who had great speed for the inside linebacker position but he was not a subtle player. Instead, he would knock a blocker or ball carrier's head off with a brutal forearm and then stand over him and snarl. He would eventually play the majority of his career at 220 pounds, but he was still regarded as an undersized player who simply could have cared less for NFL convention. He just wanted to go out and play the middle for a Steelers defense that was already among the most imposing in the league when he arrived and only got steadily better.

The image of Lambert as a raging, emotional madman leading the Steelers with his maniacal, toothless sneer has long been held by NFL fans. There were incidents to back up that image. His tossing of Dallas Cowboys defensive back Cliff Harris after Steelers place-kicker Roy Gerela missed 33-yard field goal is the stuff of legend. Harris cheekishly tapped Gerela on the helmet and told him "way to go" after the field goal sailed wide to the right. Lambert intervened. Referee Norm Schachter was about to throw Lambert out of the game for his unsportsmanlike conduct, but after hearing Lambert's defense he not only allowed him remain in the game, but decided not to throw a penalty flag.

Lambert also was called into the commissioner's office after an incident with Cleveland Browns quarterback Brian Sipe. Lambert had obliterated Sipe when the quarterback chose to stay in bounds and get extra yards instead of escaping the field of play. "I hit him as hard as I could," Lambert told commissioner Pete Rozelle. "He was in bounds. I would do the same thing again."

There were no other incidents that could be responsibly described as reckless or dirty. Instead, Lambert played the game with a great personal responsibility that impressed the Steelers' coaching staff and his teammates. Andy Russell was a linebacker with the Steelers from 1963 through 1976 and he observed Lambert's development and capabilities first hand. "Tough, raw-boned, intense," Russell told *Sports Illustrated*, "that's the way he'll be remembered, but I've seen a lot of guys like that come into the league. No, Jack's a whole lot more, The range he has . . . they put him into coverage 30 yards downfield. They gave him assignments that old Bears or Packers never would've dreamed of. He brought a whole new concept to the position, and that's why, for me anyway, he's the greatest there has ever been. His first step is never wrong, his techniques have always been perfect. His greatness has nothing to do with his popular image."

A great case can be made that the 1976 Steelers had the best defense the NFL has ever seen. They gave up only 138 points that season, 38 fewer than the Minnesota Vikings who were the runners-up in that category. The Steelers started that season with a 1–4 record before winning their final nine games. They registered five shutouts in that span, gave up six points in one other game, and three points in two others. The Steelers were the No. 1 statistical defense in the league that season, allowing 237.4 yards per game, 13 first downs per game and 104.1 rushing yards per game. They only gave up five rushing touchdowns all season, and Lambert was named the NFL's Defensive Player of the Year.

Honors came to Lambert throughout his career. He won rookie of the year in 1974, made the Pro Bowl nine times and was an All-Pro six times. But honors were not the story. He won respect in his own locker room and had an image that intimidated opponents. But more than image was the reality. Lambert took the crown of most dominant player on the most dominant defense from Greene and he wore it well.

#45

FRAN TARKENTON

Fran Tarkenton was drafted in the third round out of the University of Georgia during the Minnesota Vikings' initial draft in 1961. Even for that era, Tarkenton was considered small for the quarterback position. At an even 6 feet and 185 pounds (numbers that were likely overstated), Tarkenton had a difficult time seeing over bigger defensive linemen when protection started to break down. So he did the only logical thing. He took matters into his own hands and left the pocket when it was necessary.

Sometimes Tarkenton would scramble left and throw, sometimes he would scramble right and throw, and sometimes he would take off and run. The style was effective and thrilling to the fans, but it annoyed Vikings head coach Norm Van Brocklin, who himself had been a Hall of Fame quarterback with the Los Angeles Rams and Philadelphia Eagles. Van Brocklin thought a quarterback needed to stay in the pocket to be effective and never truly appreciated Tarkenton's gifts. These gifts were plentiful, and Tarkenton put them on display immediately. His first game was the team's debut against George Halas's powerful Chicago Bears in 1961. Instead of playing tentatively and getting pounded by their legendary opponent, Tarkenton relieved ineffective starting quarterback George Shaw early in the game and threw four touchdown passes and ran for a another to lead the Vikings to a stunning 37–13 win. No expansion team had ever had such an impressive performance in its first game, before or since.

Tarkenton was a great leader who helped make the Vikings an exciting team in their early years, even if they did suffer the normal growing pains of an expansion team. His ability to escape pressure and buy time to throw gave his receivers the chance to break containment and get open. Tarkenton made huge plays that would sometimes take 10 to 15 seconds to develop. NFL Films has reels and reels of such Tarkenton highlights at its disposal.

Tarkenton was nearly indestructible despite his small frame. He played nearly every game from 1961 through 1976 despite a slew of painful injuries that began to take their toll. However, the only serious injury he suffered in his career was a broken ankle in the 1977 season when he was hit by Cincinnati's Gary Burley. Tarkenton came back the following year, but his career came to an unceremonious end when Minnesota dropped a 34–10 decision to the Rams in the divisional playoffs.

But between his brilliant opening act and quiet finale was a brilliant 18-year career that included 13 seasons with the Vikings and five with the New York Giants. When he retired, the 1975 league MVP left holding several notable records, including most games played by a quarterback (246), most passing yards (47,003), most touchdown passes (342), most completions (3,686), most attempts (6,647), and most rushing yards by a quarterback (3,674). While Miami's Dan Marino went on to break most of these marks, all of Tarkenton's records lasted at least a decade. More than 30 years after his retirement, he still stands third all-time in touchdown passes, fifth in passing yards, eighth in completions, and fourth in rushing yards by a quarterback.

Tarkenton's style that was criticized by Van Brocklin was appreciated by his successor, Bud Grant. When Tarkenton came back to the Vikings for the final third of his career in 1972, he was a respected veteran who had suffered with some very bad Giants teams. He compiled a 33–37 record over five seasons in New York, and the team's failure to manage even one spot in the postseason frustrated Tarkenton. However, if not for his presence on the team, the Giants would have been far worse. The Giants had few other stars besides Tarkenton in those days and he earned every one of those 33 wins in New York.

By 1972, the Vikings were a full-fledged NFL power. Quarterback Gary Cuozzo had led them to 12–2 and 11–3 records in 1970 and 1971, but the Vikes had been bounced out of the playoffs in the first round by the San Francisco 49ers and Dallas Cowboys, respectively. Cuozzo was an effective quarterback, but when it came to rallying his teams and making a statement in the postseason, he simply lacked that ability. The Vikings went back to their roots and traded Norm Snead, Bob Grim, Vince Clements, and a first-round draft pick to re-acquire Tarkenton from the Giants.

It was a great move for Tarkenton, who was going from one of the saddest teams in the league to one of the most powerful. While the 1972 season was nothing special at 7–7, the Vikings would go to the playoffs the following six years with Tarkenton.

Chicago Bears linebacker Doug Buffone faced Tarkenton twice a year after his trade back to Minnesota, and the experience always left him drained. "You were never so tired after a game as when you were playing against Tarkenton," Buffone said. "He was so quick you couldn't catch him. Normally with a pocket passer, you have to cover a back or tight end two or three seconds before he gets rid of the ball. But with Tarkenton, you had to cover a guy, I don't know, five seconds or more. That's because he was running around and you could never catch him."

By buying an extraordinary amount of time, Tarkenton didn't necessarily have to zip the ball to his receiver. "He would be running around back there and you didn't know whether to stay with your guy or go after Tarkenton," Buffone said. "Enough time goes by and you go after him. He sees an open running back and he shot puts the ball over your head and he's got another completion. It was so frustrating."

The Vikings went to three Super Bowls with Tarkenton but did not win any of them. Tarkenton did not distinguish himself with his play in those games, but all three of the opponents the Vikings lost to—the Pittsburgh Steelers, Miami Dolphins, and Oakland Raiders—were legendary teams that earned a spot in NFL folklore for their accomplishments. It would have taken superhuman efforts to beat the Dolphins or Raiders, and moving the ball against Pittsburgh's "Steel Curtain" defense was nearly impossible.

Tarkenton's legacy is not one of a quarterback who started and lost three Super Bowls. It is one of innovation and creativity. His style launched a new philosophy in the NFL that is still the norm and likely to remain so for a long time. Most quarterbacks may not be able to run like Tarkenton, but they all have to buy time with their feet in order to give their receivers time to make a play.

RUSHING YARDS BY QUARTERBACKS (THROUGH 2013 SEASON)				
PLAYER	ATT	YDS	Y/A	TD
1. Michael Vick	827	5857	7.1	36
2. Randall Cunningham	775	4928	6.4	35
3. Steve Young	722	4239	5.9	43
4. Fran Tarkenton	675	3674	5.4	32
5. Steve McNair	669	3590	5.4	37

#46

O. J. SIMPSON

It was a lifetime ago. Or two lifetimes ago. Long before O. J. Simpson became a pivotal figure in America's debate over race relations and was accused of the double murder of his ex-wife and her friend, there was a time when O. J. Simpson was perhaps the best football player in the world. After a Heisman Trophy–winning career at USC, a world-class smile and a bevy of highlight-film runs, the Buffalo Bills made Heisman Trophy winner O. J. Simpson the first overall pick in the 1969 NFL draft.

Simpson would go on to become a record-breaking runner in the NFL, but not before some difficulties in his early years. For one, Buffalo head coach John Rauch was hesitant to let Simpson take over as the team's featured back in his offense. It was a frustrating time for Simpson, who looked like an average back in the Buffalo scheme.

But pro football fans finally saw what Simpson was capable of when Lou Saban took over as head coach in 1972. Buffalo owner Ralph Wilson had been tired of the way coaches had kept the wraps on Simpson. He told Saban to let Simpson run.

When Saban met with Simpson, he told him that he was planning to let the running back run the way he had when he was at the University of Southern California. Simpson became the happiest man in western New York after that conversation and his subsequent running helped the Bills become a viable force in the NFL. The 1972 season was Simpson's coming-out party. After looking over his shoulder for the first three years of his career as if waiting to be taken out of the game, Simpson started to run free and easy for the first time since he had been a dominating college star. "The Juice" ran for a league-high 1,251 yards in 1972 while averaging a respectable 4.3 yards per carry. He had six rushing touchdowns, including a shocking 94-yarder that would prove to be the long play of his career.

Simpson liked his role in the Saban offense and promised Buffalo fans that what they had seen was just the beginning of what he would accomplish throughout his career. Simpson knew he was on the verge of accomplishing some memorable feats with the great offensive line built by Saban with Hall of Famer Joe Delammie-lure and Reggie McKenzie, a unit dubbed "The Electric Company" because "it turned on the Juice."

Simpson went from star to legend the next season. The NFL was still playing a 14-game schedule in 1973, yet Simpson carried 332 times for 2,003 yards and 12 touchdowns, capturing league MVP honors. He averaged 6.0 yards per carry and was simply too fast and quick for defenses trying to slow him down. He became the first player to rush for 2,000 yards in an NFL season and would hold the record for most rushing yards in a season until Eric Dickerson ran for 2,105 yards 11 years later.

Simpson took great pride in his accomplishment. "No matter what happens to me, I was the first man to rush for 2,000 yards in a season," Simpson said. "They can never take that away from me." Simpson was the only player to rush for 2,000 yards in a 14-game season.

He needed two spectacular games at the end of the season to reach the mark. In Week 13, Simpson carried 22 times for 219 yards against the New England Patriots in a 37–13 Buffalo victory. The following week, he carried 34 times for 200 yards in the snow at Shea Stadium against the New York Jets in a 34–14 Buffalo victory.

Two years later—another 14-game season—Simpson was nearly as good. He carried 329 times for 1,817 yards with 16 touchdowns and averaged 5.5 yards per carry. He also scored seven more touchdowns as a receiver, setting an NFL record for touchdowns in a season. He followed that season with 1,503 yards in 1976, averaging 5.2 yards per carry and rushing for eight touchdowns.

Over a five-year period from 1972 through 1976, Simpson averaged 1,540 yards per season and led the league in rushing four times. He also averaged nine touchdowns per season over that span. It was a sensational five-year run, nearly as good as LaDainian Tomlinson would post three decades later. Injuries would later take their toll on the six-time Pro Bowler, however, and he had little left in the tank when he finished his career with the San Francisco 49ers in 1978 and 1979.

After his career ended, Simpson made movies and served as an analyst on NFL broadcasts. The word that was used to describe his personality was "affable."

That would all change in June 1994 with the double murder of Nicole Brown and Ronald Goldman. Though he was acquitted of the murders, Simpson's momentous achievements on the field were replaced in the collective American memory by what was perceived to be his monstrous activity off of it.

O. J. Simpson

Rank	Player	Team	Year	Yards
1	Eric Dickerson	L.A. Rams	1984	2,105
2	Adrian Peterson	Minn.	2012	2,097
3	Jamal Lewis	Baltimore	2003	2,066
4	Barry Sanders	Detroit	1997	2,053
5	Terrell Davis	Denver	1998	2,008
6	Chris Johnson	Tenn.	2009	2,006
7	O.J. Simpson	Buff.	1973	2,003

2,000-YARD RUSHING SEASONS

#47

WILLIE DAVIS

The most important member of Green Bay's defensive line during the Vince Lombardi era was not happy about being traded to the Packers. Drafted by the Cleveland Browns in 1956, Davis's football career didn't get underway until 1958 because he had a military obligation to fulfill. When he finally got a chance to play, he was used at various positions along the offensive line by the Browns and didn't necessarily fit in with their long-term plans. As a result, he was traded to Green Bay in 1960, a move that Davis did not exactly welcome.

At the time, Green Bay was not an easy place to live for an African-American player. Aside from the players on the Packers, the number of African-Americans living in Green Bay and the surrounding area was negligible. With the Packers not even a blip on the NFL radar, Davis thought about quitting football and going on to the business world. Davis didn't know much about their head coach Vince Lombardi, who had just completed his first year with the Packers. Davis didn't know much about Lombardi even though he had been one of the key assistants on Jim Lee Howell's New York Giants staff (along with Tom Landry). That the Packers had gone 7–5 in Lombardi's first season didn't impress him, even though it was the most wins in Green Bay since 1944.

However, Davis decided to speak with Lombardi before making any decision about his career. Lombardi told Davis that there would be no more jumping around from position to position on the offensive line and instead he would play defensive end for the Packers. "I consider speed, agility, and size to be the three most important attributes in a successful lineman," Lombardi told Davis. "Give me a man who has any two of those dimensions and he'll do okay. But give him all three and he'll be great. We think you have all three."

That was sufficient for Davis to put his post-football career on hold. He became a dominating performer for the Packers, a relentless pass rusher who was also dominant against the run. Lombardi had had high hopes for Davis but he exceeded them in every way possible. Lombardi had expected him to make big plays and he did, but he also became one of the leaders on the defensive side of the ball and had a calming effect on his teammates in tight situations. The team got plenty of passion from middle linebacker Ray Nitschke, and cornerback Willie Wood was a scintillating athlete who had an instinct for the interception and could shut down receivers, but it was Davis who the team looked to in clutch situations.

The Packers would begin their championship run in 1961, going 11–3 and thrashing the Giants 37–0 in the NFL Championship Game. They had the No. 2 defense in the league that season and would finish no worse than second in defense in the league for the next six seasons. While that consistency was impressive, what the Packers did in 1966 was striking. They finished the season ranked first in points allowed (163) and passing yards allowed (1,959) while surrendering only seven touchdown passes against 28 interceptions.

"It was a remarkable year for the Packers defense and the thing I remember most is that no quarterback we faced ever had time to pass," said Packers guard Jerry Kramer. "It was like Willie was in the backfield all season. He was either sacking the quarterback, pressuring him or knocking a pass away. It was almost impossible to block him."

In 1967, the Packers were in the final year of their three-year championship run. They had beaten the Rams in the first round of the playoffs and then faced the Cowboys in the famed "Ice Bowl" for the NFL championship. The Packers won the game on Bart Starr's 1-yard quarterback sneak for a touchdown in sub-arctic conditions on the game's final play, one that Davis couldn't even watch. "I was thinking of everything that could go wrong on that play," Davis explained. "The snap, the block, a fumble—anything could have happened. I couldn't watch. Thankfully, the crowd let us know what happened. I wasn't the only defensive player who couldn't watch."

The move to Green Bay turned out to be the pivotal move for Davis, who would win All-Pro honors five times in his career and earn a spot in the Hall of Fame in 1981.

#48

MARSHALL FAULK

When Marshall Faulk came out of San Diego State and was taken with the second pick in the 1994 draft by the Indianapolis Colts, the scouts around the NFL were in near unanimity about his chances for success. His speed, ability to run with the football and talent as a pass catcher made him a can't-miss player.

The numbers say that's exactly what Faulk was as a rookie. He ran for 1,282 yards, scored 11 touchdowns and averaged 4.1 yards per carry while hauling in 52 receptions for 522 yards and a touchdown. Faulk quickly established himself as the dual threat he would prove to be throughout his career.

But he also got a reputation for being a selfish player. Some of it may have been jealousy from some of his teammates, but Faulk is the first to admit that he was concerned with his own numbers. "It wasn't that I was selfish," Faulk explained. "But I was always a very goal-oriented individual. Achieving things on the football field was important to me and some may have taken it the wrong way. I always wanted to win and that was my top priority, but I also wanted to hold up my end."

Faulk had four seasons in which he rushed for 1,000 yards or more during his five years with the Indianapolis Colts. He was also a dominant receiver, catching 86 balls in 1998, his final year with the team. Faulk took pride in every aspect of the game and was a very good blocker.

But following a game against the Baltimore Ravens in 1998, Faulk realized he was playing with the wrong attitude. In the game, a 38-31 Raven win over the Colts, Faulk ran for 192 yards and caught seven passes for 75 yards. He caught a 34-yard TD pass from Peyton Manning in the first quarter and ran for a 68-yard touchdown on the Colts next possession. However, with the Colts on a late, fourth-quarter drive that would have allowed them to tie the game, Faulk made an error. He went out for a flare pass from Manning and lost concentration as the ball flew to him and it deflected off his hands. The ball was intercepted and the Ravens closed out the game.

After the game, Faulk was feeling pretty good because the 192 rushing yards was his career high. He had obviously had a monster statistical game, but that did not impress head coach Jim Mora. The deflected pass had turned into the game-losing play and Mora let Faulk hear it in front of the team.

Faulk used that moment as the turning point in his career. He realized he was not as team-oriented as he could be and vowed to change that. The Colts would trade Faulk to the St. Louis Rams in the offseason and he used his new environment to show both the Rams and himself that he had to do everything he could to help the team win and not just accumulate statistics.

"Jim Mora was right. I dropped the pass and it was my fault," Faulk said. "There was more I could have done to help my team. I made it a point that everything I did from that point forward was going to help my team."

That first season in St. Louis saw the Rams win the Super Bowl. Talk about instantaneous results. "We knew we were getting an outstanding football player," said St. Louis head coach Dick Vermeil. "We knew Marshall was a great runner and a great receiver who could make a difference in every game. But we didn't know how good he really was. The way he prepared himself and his dedication showed that he was going to do anything he could to make his team successful."

That first season with the Rams saw Faulk rush for 1,381 yards and seven touchdowns. He also caught 87 passes for 1,048 yards and became only the second player in NFL history (Roger Craig was the first) to run for 1,000 or more yards and catch at least 1,000 yards worth of passes in the same season.

Faulk would put his best numbers on the board in the 2000 season. He rushed for 1,359 yards and 18 touchdowns and caught 81 passes for 830 yards and eight touchdowns. It was one of the most remarkable seasons in league history and Rams head coach Mike Martz, who had taken over for Vermeil after the Super Bowl win, was amazed by Faulk's knowledge of the game. "You hear the phrase 'coach on the field,'" Martz explained. "That's just what Marshall was for us. Not only could he tell you what happened on a play, he could come up with a fix almost immediately if the play went wrong."

That's the kind of attitude and determination with which Faulk would play the remaining years of his career. It was something that Faulk took a lot of pride in but few people outside the locker room ever knew about. "I always felt I got tagged with this attitude of being a natural athlete," Faulk explained. "But I was a student of the game and nobody realized the kind of technical knowledge I had. I took a lot of pride in that."

By the time he retired at the end of the 2005 season, the seven-time Pro Bowler had rushed for 12,279 yards and averaged 4.3 yards per carry. He also caught 767 passes for 6,875 yards, averaging 9.0 yards per reception. As of the writing of this book, Faulk's 19,154 yards from scrimmage are fourth-best in league history and his 136 total touchdowns rank him sixth all-time. Those numbers were enough to satisfy a very "goal-oriented" performer, but he had become one of the most team-oriented players in the league throughout his run in St. Louis.

MOST SEASONS WITH 2,000 COMBINED YARDS FROM SCRIMMAGE

Player	Team	Years
Eric Dickerson	RAMS-IND	4
Marshall Faulk	IND-STL	4
Walter Payton	CHI	4
Tiki Barber	NYG	3
Priest Holmes	KC	3
LaDainian Tomlinson	SD	3

#49

ROD WOODSON

There was no doubt from the moment he stepped on an NFL field that Rod Woodson was going to do his job.

Woodson, however, had many jobs. The first of which was shutting down opposing receivers. He could play physically at the line of scrimmage or he could play the trail technique and goad a quarterback into thinking the receiver was open, throwing the pass so Woodson could then intercept it. He could also play straight coverage, handle multiple moves, and stay with the receiver step for step.

Woodson didn't stop there, though. He was a first-rate tackler in the running game and one of the top kick returners of his era. After a long run as an All-Pro cornerback, Woodson switched to safety and closed out his career there. In addition to being one of the best cornerbacks the game has known, Woodson was also one of the best safeties.

In his 17 NFL seasons with the Pittsburgh Steelers (1987–1996), San Francisco 49ers (1997), Baltimore Ravens (1998–2001), and Oakland Raiders (2002–2003) Woodson recorded 71 interceptions (third all-time), 1,483 interception return yards (first all-time), 2,362 punt return yards, and 17 non-offensive touchdowns (second all-time). He also reached the end zone on an NFL-record 12 interception returns (first all-time), one fumble return, two punt returns, and two kickoff returns. Woodson, a member of the 1990s All-Decade Team, was named to the Pro Bowl 11 times (a record for defensive backs) and in 1994—after just seven years as an NFL corner—was one of just five active players to be named to the NFL's 75th Anniversary Team. The others were Jerry Rice, Joe Montana, Reggie White, and Ronnie Lott.

The 10th overall pick in the 1987 NFL Draft (out of Purdue University), Woodson enjoyed the fact that he came of age in the NFL when pass coverage was far more physical than it is today. In the rare event that he was beaten for a few steps, Woodson was not averse to putting his hands on a receiver. "If they ran by you, you could push them and slow 'em up, so how could you ever get beat deep?" he asked. "Wouldn't that be fun? You could terrify receivers."

But as the years went by and defensive backs faced more and more restrictions, Woodson made every adjustment he needed to and rarely lost any of his battles. He set a tone for the Steelers (and later on for the 49ers, Ravens, and Raiders) that his teammates took note of.

"It's crazy," said Steelers cornerback D.J. Johnson in 1994. "You can't touch a receiver or it's a flag, and they can do anything they want to get open. You have to depend on a great pass rush and some liberal referees. For Rod to do what he is doing, it is simply spectacular. How can you guard a guy that close, tip the ball, or make an interception on every play and not be called for a penalty? It just takes outstanding athletic ability."

After Woodson made back-to-back Pro Bowls in 1992 and 1993, opponents started to recognize his ability to make plays and started scheming against him. They refrained from throwing to his side of the field for fear that he would intercept the ball or force a fumble. Steelers head coach Bill Cowher changed Woodson's role and made him a hybrid cornerback/safety so he could find the ball and make plays even if the receiver he was covering was not involved in the play.

Cowher's instructions were not necessarily specific. He just told Woodson in his inimitable jaw-jutting, spit-flying style that he needed to find the ball and make plays. "He kind of thrives on that and has taken his game to another level," Cowher said. "You have to try to get him around the football as much as you can. If you leave him in one spot, they can scheme away from him. We want him involved."

Woodson said that when he came into his own with the Steelers, it was the combination of his experience, athletic ability, and the coaching of defensive coordinator Dick LeBeau that turned him into one of the best all-around defensive players the game has ever seen. "Coach LeBeau was such a stickler for technique," Woodson said. "He knew what we needed to do and he excelled at teaching us. We did it the right way. We played our system and kept up all our responsibilities. We stayed on the outside shoulder of the receiver, and we didn't freelance."

Woodson would have had a memorable career if it ended during the 1995 season, when an anterior-cruciate-ligament injury sidelined him and threatened the end of his playing days. He did not have the same quickness when he came back but he moved to free safety and became one of the best at that position when he played with the 49ers, Ravens, and Raiders.

His most memorable season during that second portion of his career came in 2000, his third season with the Ravens. That year,

Baltimore won the championship with the best defense the league had seen since the 1985 Bears. Middle linebacker Ray Lewis was in the prime of his career and clearly the unit's best player and leader, but Lewis was one of the first to acknowledge how much Woodson meant to the team at free safety. Woodson's 77 tackles, two forced fumbles, three fumble recoveries, and four interceptions gave Baltimore's sack-oriented and hard-charging defense the confidence that if the pass rushers didn't get to the quarterback, Woodson would make the play in the secondary.

He would play three more years and make one more All-Pro team in 2002 and then call it a career. He was a dominant player in the beginning, the middle, and the end. Before knee surgery and after. One of a kind.

INTERCEPTION RETURN YARDS LEADERS (THROUGH 2013 SEASON)

Rank	Player	Years	Interception return yards
1	Ed Reed	2002-2013	1,590
2	Rod Woodson	1987-2003	1,483
3	Darren Sharper	1997-2008	1,412
4	Deion Sanders	1989-2005	1,331
5	Emlen Tunnell	1948-1961	1,282
6	Dick "Night Train" Lane	1952-1965	1,207
7	Paul Krause	1964-1979	1,185
9	Lem Barney	1967-1977	1,077
9	Herb Adderley	1961-1972	1,046
10	Bobby Boyd	1960-1968	994

#50

JOHN MACKEY

John Mackey was a difference maker for the Baltimore Colts.

When Mackey stepped onto the field in a Colts uniform in 1963, it didn't take Johnny Unitas long to realize he had a weapon who could light up the scoreboard. Unitas may not have understood the position Mackey was playing, but he saw a big, fast, and strong, man who could run downfield from the tight end position and make big plays for the Colts.

Prior to the arrival of Mackey with the Baltimore Colts and Mike Ditka with the Chicago Bears (two years earlier), the position of tight end was nothing more than a glorified offensive tackle.

Perhaps the tight end would catch one pass per game or more likely, one pass every other game. The main job of the tight end was to block for the running game and get downfield in the passing game and block for a wide receiver or flanker back who happened to get fairly deep.

The presence of the 6-2, 224-pound Mackey changed that. When he put on his familiar No. 88 jersey for the Colts, Mackey could block in the running game and also help keep Unitas upright when he settled into the pocket.

However, Mackey was capable of so much more. He was an outstanding route runner who could get open on short- and medium-range passes. He could stiff-arm his way out of tackles and continue to make big yardage as he ran around and over linebackers and defensive backs.

Mackey could also get deep. He had the kind of quickness and speed that allowed him to torment opposing defensive coaches with downfield catches from a position that rarely—if ever—delivered those plays.

His first season with the Colts was an eye opener. He caught 35 passes for 726 yards and seven touchdowns. While 35 receptions in a 14-game season doesn't sound like much in 2014, it was a huge number for tight ends in the early 1960s.

But it was the yardage total that caused most of the problems. Mackey averaged 20.7 yards that season, and it was his speed that made the difference. He ran a 4.6 40 when he came out of Syracuse and joined the Colts, and a rookie coach named Don Shula was not afraid to change the job description for the tight end position.

Shula recognized that Mackey was faster than most of the defensive backs the Colts had, as he gave them a very difficult time in training camp and practice. As a result, Shula knew he could alter the Colts' game plan, give Unitas a dynamic new weapon, and help the Colts become a legitimate NFL power once again.

Not only would Unitas put the ball in a spot that only Mackey could reach, but also he excelled at setting up the defense to exploit his tight end's ability to make a big play at the key moment in the game.

"John could get open and make the big play," Unitas said. "I could always count on him to get open at the big moment. I wanted to throw to him when the game was on the line. He would always catch it."

The Colts finished 8-6 in 1963, and they finished in third place in the Western Conference behind the eventual champion Chicago Bears and the Green Bay Packers.

That was just the beginning of their climb. The Colts became something of a juggernaut in 1964, as they rolled to a 12-2 season.

Thanks in large part to Mackey, the Colts were nearly unstoppable on the offensive side of the ball as they scored a league-high 428 points that season. Mackey caught 22-406-2 that season, but he had served notice the previous year, and opponents had to look out for him on every play. That gave Unitas a number of options every time the Colts had the ball, and the all-time great quarterback took advantage of them on an every-week basis.

The Colts were upset in the NFL championship game by the Cleveland Browns that season, but they would remain a winning team in each of Mackey's nine seasons with the team.

The Baltimore Colts would win their only Super Bowl following the 1970 season when they defeated the Dallas Cowboys 16-13. While that Super Bowl became known as the "Blunder Bowl" because the two teams combined for 11 turnovers—still a record—it was Mackey who caught a 75-yard touchdown pass from Unitas in the second quarter that allowed the Colts to tie the game.

Off the field, Mackey would also become an unsung hero when he successfully challenged the "Rozelle Rule" in court. The Rozelle Rule required any team that signed another team's free agent to pay compensation for the lost player, and it had a chilling effect on the signing of free agents within the league.

By winning that case, Mackey became a driving force for players who desperately sought free agency. The political ramifications of his stand also delayed his entry into the Hall of Fame, but he got there in 1992, 20 years after his playing career ended.

Mackey's latter years were marked by a cruel battle with dementia, something he endured from 2000 until he died in 2011. Mackey's struggles were a driving force in the NFL–NFLPA negotiations that increased the pension for players suffering from dementia from $30,000 to $88,000 per year.

Mackey's contributions on and off the field have been wide-ranging and consequential. Few players have ever matched his impact.

#51

TONY DORSETT

The Dallas Cowboys were on a roll in the 1970s, winning two Super Bowls and making the playoffs in every year of the decade except 1974. However, going into the 1977 draft, there was something missing from their offense.

Despite their success, the Cowboys had become somewhat predictable. Roger Staubach could still throw the ball and Drew Pearson was one of the best receivers in the league, but Tom Landry did not have an explosive running back. Both Landry and general manager Tex Schramm knew the Cowboys needed more fire out of the backfield and they saw a player who could help them in the 1977 draft. Heisman Trophy winner Tony Dorsett had all the speed and explosiveness that had been missing from the Cowboy attack. The problem was that the Cowboys were picking 24th in the first round and had no chance at the University of Pittsburgh star.

But Schramm and Landry decided to pay the price to move up. They traded up with Seattle, giving the Seahawks a first-round pick and three second-round choices for the right to the second overall pick. After the Tampa Bay Buccaneers chose USC running back Ricky Bell with the top pick, the Cowboys took Dorsett and never looked back.

The Dallas pre-draft analysis had been correct. Dorsett possessed all of the ingredients they had been missing and after playing for the Pitt team that won the national championship in 1976, Dorsett played a key role for the Cowboys team that won the Super Bowl championship in his rookie season. Dorsett ran for 1,007 yards and won the Offensive Rookie of the Year Award. Having great speed and knowing how to use it to his advantage were his keys in both his rookie season and throughout his career.

"After winning the national championship at Pitt in my senior year and then moving to the Cowboys as a rookie, I just felt good things were going to happen," Dorsett said. "I thought before I got to camp that we had a good chance to win the Super Bowl. After all this was the Cowboys with Roger Staubach and Tom Landry and the "Doomsday Defense." And now they had me. It just seemed like we had a great chance."

It was more than a chance. The 1977 Cowboys rolled to a 12–2 record, punished the Chicago Bears and Minnesota Vikings in the NFC playoffs and then dominated the Denver Broncos in Super Bowl XII in New Orleans, 27–10. "It was the best feeling of my pro football career," Dorsett said. "When you win the Super Bowl as a rookie it's just an awesome feeling. It's not that you think you're automatically going to win every year, but when you play on that team you know you are going to have a fighting chance."

Dorsett's presence made life much easier for Staubach. In 1976, Staubach had thrown 14 touchdown passes and 11 interceptions.

With Dorsett averaging 4.8 yards per carry and scoring 12 rushing touchdowns, Staubach found more open passing lanes in 1977. His touchdown-to-interception ratio improved to 18 to 9. Drew Pearson and backup running back Preston Pearson (no relation) combined for 94 receptions and six touchdowns.

His rookie season turned out to be the only time in his pro career that Dorsett won a Super Bowl, but he piled up honors and awards throughout his career. He was a four-time Pro Bowler, a three-time All-NFC selection and he ran for 12,739 yards in his 11-year career (seventh all-time as of the writing of this book) before being inducted into the Hall of Fame in 1993.

Staubach was thrilled with the decision to draft Dorsett and had no problems with the $1.1 million contract Dorsett signed even though the quarterback was making only $250,000 at the time. "We needed Tony Dorsett when we drafted him," Staubach said. "We really hadn't had much of a running game before he got there. Once he arrived, the feeling was that we didn't have any major holes.

"A lot of people thought the money he signed for would cause problems, but I had no problems. They could have paid him double as long as we won the Super Bowl and that's just what happened."

Dorsett played much of his career with a chip on his shoulder. Before he was drafted and even as he was finding success in his career, he heard whispers about his size. Skeptics thought he was too small and too skinny to make it.

"That really got to me," said Dorsett, who played at 5-foot-11 and 185 pounds. "It motivated me. Any time I heard that I was not big enough to be an effective NFL running back I wanted to make somebody pay. It was never about size. It was about how much you were willing to fight and the talent you had. All I knew was that I was going to get the most out of what I had."

Landry had his own fears about Dorsett's size. He knew he had a great back on his hands, but Dorsett was not as big or strong as Houston's Earl Campbell. "I was not going to use Tony the way the

Oilers used Campbell," Landry explained. "I wanted him to have a long career and not take so much abuse that he would get hurt. I think it worked out pretty well for him and for us."

Dorsett's most notable play took place during the 1982 season in the regular-season finale at Minnesota on a Monday night. In that game, Dorsett took a handoff from Cowboys quarterback Danny White at the Dallas 1 yard line and ran 99 yards for a touchdown. Making it even more memorable is that the Cowboys had only 10 men on the field because running back Ron Springs did not realize he was supposed to be on the field for that third-down play and was watching from the bench.

"That's the play that I am asked about more than any other one in my career," Dorsett said. "I just got the ball, ran the play, and there it was. I'm not saying it was my best run but it was definitely my most memorable."

#52

ED REED

In many ways, Ed Reed was more like an NBA player who just happened to play football.

In the NBA, teams often get their offense going by playing spectacularly on the defensive end. A steal, a blocked shot, and a deflected pass are all tools that can jumpstart an NBA offense.

Reed often used all of those tools and more to get the Baltimore Ravens going when he was in the heyday of his career. Reed combined top-level athleticism, excellent instincts, and a notion for physical play with maximum leadership ability.

Together, with middle linebacker Ray Lewis, he helped the Ravens play formidable defense on an every-week basis.

Reed was drafted in the first round (24th pick overall) out of Miami in 2002. He immediately became a starter on the Ravens defense, fitting right in at strong safety. Reed would also play many years at the more-instinctive free safety position, but he was such a hard and aggressive hitter that he was also a natural fit at the strong safety position.

Reed became a big-time player in his first season, and he immediately showed a knack for making game-changing plays. He had five interceptions in that first season, and he also had 12 pass deflections to go along with 85 tackles. More than the numbers, Reed showed the tendency to be in the right place at the right time.

His instincts gave him a good feel to understand what the opposing quarterback and offensive coordinator wanted to do next, and he was regularly able to put himself in a position to make a game-changing play.

He served notice the following year that he was going to become one of the top defensive backs in the game. Reed made the Pro Bowl for the first time, as he had seven interceptions that he returned for 154 yards and a touchdown, 15 passes defensed, 73 tackles and one forced fumble. During the 2003 season, the ever-alert Reed showed his remarkable ability to flash to the ball, make a spectacular catch, and then turn defense into offense with a long return.

Reed was productive as a rookie and elite as a second-year player. However, he came into his own during the 2004 season when he was named the Associated Press Defensive Player of the Year. Reed did everything that head coach Brian Billick asked of him, and then a little bit more. Reed was a ball hawk on the field, as it seemed like he had a chance to come away with the interception on nearly every pass that was thrown in the Ravens' secondary.

Reed had nine interceptions that he returned for 358 yards and a touchdown, and he also had 17 passes defensed. Reed's hard hitting also became a huge factor, as he forced three fumbles, recovered two more, and returned one of them for a touchdown. He registered 76 tackles that season.

Ed Reed

The highlight was Reed's a 106-yard interception return for a touchdown against the Cleveland Browns that clinched that Week Nine victory. The Ravens were leading the Browns 20-13 in the late stages of the fourth quarter, when the Browns attempted to tie the score behind veteran quarterback Jeff Garcia. The former 49er tried to squeeze in a game-tying touchdown pass, but the instant he released the ball, Reed drove on the football, intercepted it deep in the end zone, and sped away on a remarkable run that decided the game in the Ravens' favor.

From that point on his career, Reed became known for his ability as a remarkable open-field runner. When he got his hands on the ball as a result of an interception, fumble recovery, blocked punt, or taking a lateral from a teammate, Reed knew how to make things happen.

"When Ed had the ball it was always exciting," Billick said. "He didn't always go all the way, but if he had the ball in his hands, you knew he was capable of scoring. Some guys think the play is over after they intercept the ball. They want to head out of bounds or get down on the ground without fumbling. With Ed Reed, the play was just starting when he intercepted the ball."

The Ravens tried to compete for years by playing hard-hitting and nasty defense with Lewis and Reed providing the leadership. While cameras and the media often focused on the remarkable linebacker for his speeches and trademark pregame dance, Reed was often the team's rallying point.

His ability to come up with huge plays was perhaps his signature during his 11-year run with the Ravens from 2002 through 2012. He led the NFL in interceptions three times, and he scored seven touchdowns while returning those interceptions. He also had two more touchdown returns while bringing back fumble recoveries.

As good as he was during the regular season, he was even more valuable during the playoffs. Reed holds the NFL record with nine postseason interceptions.

Reed also became one of the most valuable special-teams players in the game's history. He was perhaps its best punt blocker, as he returned three blocked punts for touchdowns in his career. Reed is the only player in NFL history to return an interception, a punt, a fumble, and a blocked punt for touchdowns.

Reed's awareness on the field gave the team the presence of a coach. However, no coach could ever sprint or break tackles the way Reed could when he had the ball under his arm.

"I have always enjoyed studying film," Reed said. "It helps me to get to know who I'm playing against and what they like to do on the field. But I wasn't just looking at film for something to do. I was doing it so I could plan my next move and figure out how to attack."

Few players ever did more when it came to creating offense from defense. He is one of the most instinctive players to man both the strong and free safety positions, and his game-changing talents made him one of the NFL's most important players.

#53

MIKE DITKA

Some may know him as the sleepy analyst who pontificates while doing a pregame show every Sunday on ESPN. Others may know him as a pitchman who has hustled every product offered to him.

Even more know him as head coach of the 1985 Chicago Bears, one of the NFL's most legendary teams. That Bears team marauded through the NFL with a 15-1 regular-season record and then won the only Super Bowl in the team's history. The 1985 Bears are often looked at as the greatest one-season champion in NFL history.

But before he became a coach and a personality, Mike Ditka was one of the most important players in NFL history. He basically invented the modern tight end position.

Ditka was a powerful player who could muscle and punish when he was asked to block. He came to the Bears as a much-celebrated tight end out of Pittsburgh in 1961 as the fifth overall pick in the draft, and head coach George Halas saw that Ditka was a far greater receiving weapon than the NFL had ever seen at the tight end position. In addition to his toughness, Ditka had the speed to get downfield, knew how to get open, and didn't drop the ball when he got his hands on it.

He caught 56 passes for 1,076 yards and 12 touchdowns in his rookie season, starting a run of four straight seasons as the best tight end in the game. He was the team's best offensive weapon during their 1963 championship season, catching 59 passes for 794 yards and 8 touchdowns.

Ditka credited Halas with helping to make him the team's key receiver. Many expected Ditka to become a linebacker because of his size and strength, but Halas decided to break the mold and turn tight end into a position that could produce big offensive numbers.

Halas, one of the game's founding fathers, was never known for his visionary ideas. But in this case, he saw a player who had the speed, hand-eye coordination, and talent to make big plays from a position that had rarely been used for anything but blocking.

Ditka would remain one of the team's major offensive forces for the next four seasons, and he was on top of his game during the 1963 season. The Bears were largely a defensive juggernaut that year, but Ditka was able to give them a spark that season with 59 receptions for 794 yards and eight touchdowns.

He made the most famous play of his career that season. The Bears were playing the Pittsburgh Steelers November 24, two days after President John F. Kennedy was assassinated. While NFL commissioner Pete Rozelle would face intense criticism for allowing games to be played that day, Ditka would make the most of it.

With the Bears trailing the Pittsburgh Steelers 17-14 late in the fourth quarter, Ditka took a short pass on a 3rd-and-33 play, and he started chugging upfield. Ditka was hit full force by five different Steeler defenders but he did not go down until he had gained 63 yards. The Bears tied the game on a field goal, and that was a vital development as they were able to maintain their lead over the Green Bay Packers in the NFL's Western Conference.

Ditka would play through the 1972 season. Halas traded him to the Eagles after the 1966 season, and he had two miserable years in Philadelphia before resurrecting his career with Tom Landry and the Dallas Cowboys. While Halas would undoubtedly be the biggest influence in Ditka's football career, Landry was a close second. He caught 30 passes for 371 yards in the Cowboys' Super Bowl season of 1971, and he caught a touchdown pass from Roger Staubach in Super Bowl VI. Ditka's desire to become a coach may have started as a player under Halas, but he learned the intricacies of the profession from Landry.

Ditka's early years with the Bears are highly underrated. Not only was he incredibly productive at his position, but also he did it with the most pedestrian of quarterbacks throwing him the ball. Billy Wade and Rudy Bukich had plenty of heart and toughness, but neither one could throw the ball more than 20 yards without some kind of wobble. To average 62 receptions with those two at quarterback speaks of Ditka's fire, ability to get open, and competitive streak.

Ditka became the first tight end inducted into the Pro Football Hall of Fame. While generations of fans would know him as a coach, analyst, and pitchman, Ditka's ability to carve out a niche for himself at a position that was largely ignored before he got there makes him one of the most influential players in the game's history.

#54

TONY GONZALEZ

Tony Gonzalez was the rarest of commodities in the NFL. He finished his career on his own terms.

He left the game following the 2013 season, having played and started all 16 games with the Falcons throughout the season. There was nothing new about that. Gonzalez missed just two games in his career, and after coming off the bench all 16 games as a rookie, he started every game throughout the rest of his career.

Playing 17 years in the NFL and remaining relatively healthy throughout is quite remarkable, but it doesn't begin to explain how effective Gonzalez was for the Kansas City Chiefs and the Atlanta Falcons.

Gonzalez spent the first 12 years of his career as a brilliant pass catcher for the Chiefs from the tight end position and did not miss a beat after he was traded to the Falcons. He was just as slick in his later years as he was during his prime.

If Mike Ditka and John Mackey set the bar for future NFL tight ends, nobody raised it higher than Gonzalez. He not only finished his career as the top receiving tight end in the game's history, but also he is the No. 2 all-time receiver behind Jerry Rice.

Gonzalez finished his career with 1,325 receptions for 15,127 yards and 111 touchdowns. He has 223 more receptions than wide receiver Marvin Harrison, who ranks third all-time in catches.

If you want to compare him to other tight ends, he has simply lapped the field. Jason Witten of the Dallas Cowboys, who is still an active player at the dawn of the 2014 season, is second with 879 receptions.

His yardage and touchdown totals are records for tight ends.

Here are some of Gonzalez's more notable achievements:

- First tight end to exceed 15,000 receiving yards.
- Most seasons with 1,000 receiving yards by a tight end (four).
- Most consecutive seasons with 60-plus receptions (15).
- Most consecutive seasons with 70-plus receptions (11).
- Most Pro Bowl selections for a tight end (14)

Gonzalez played the game at a faster pace than most of his peers at the position. He had the quickness, athleticism, and leaping ability of a basketball star, a career that Gonzalez had pursued as a college athlete at the University of California, Berkeley.

He was a remarkably gifted player, and when the Chiefs drafted him in 1997 with the 13th pick, they were expecting to get a superstar.

However, Gonzalez did not play like a superstar right away. When he met the media at his introductory press conference, he told reporters that he liked to have fun.

When a good-looking player like Gonzalez is talking about enjoying himself off the field, there may be questions about his work ethic and his desire to succeed.

Gonzalez did not answer those questions in his rookie year, when he caught 33 passes. He did not answer them in his second year, when he caught 59 passes. While he had shown some improvement, he dropped an incredible number of passes. There were a lot of issues with his game, and Gonzalez knew that he was not playing up to his talent level.

He rededicated himself to his craft—catching passes—during the offseason. Gonzalez would catch hundreds of balls per day from that point forward, because he did not want to be just another highly paid player who produced sometimes. He wanted to achieve greatness.

Actually, Gonzalez's goal was to reach his full potential as a person, and that certainly meant more than just achieving on the football field. But becoming a great professional was certainly a part of his goal. To reach that level, he had to develop his talent fully and become the best player he could possibly be.

It was all about working hard at honing his craft. He caught 76 passes in his third year and became a star, but Gonzalez was not satisfied. He wanted to keep pushing himself every year and striving to reach the highest level.

No matter how many passes Gonzalez caught, he always wanted more. It was the part of the game he enjoyed the most and it was all about working to get better.

As good of a pass catcher as he was, he never shied away from the rough-and-tumble requirements of the position. He was a hard-working and talented blocker. He was bigger, stronger, and faster than many of his opponents, but he was also smarter. Not only could he dominate them physically, but also he could set them up so he could register effective block after effective block.

Unfortunately for Gonzalez, he never got to a Super Bowl. He only came close once.

In 2012, the Falcons had a superb year, as they were 13-3 during the regular season. They were the top-seeded team in the NFC and they edged the Seattle Seahawks in the divisional playoffs. However, they dropped a devastating 28-24 decision to the San Francisco 49ers in the NFC Championship game.

A heartbroken Gonzalez decided to play one more year with the hope that the Falcons were on the cusp of a championship, but injuries keyed a brutal 4-12 season.

Gonzalez never got the glory that comes with a championship run, but he is perhaps the greatest athlete to play the position, and it will likely be many years before any tight end approaches his achievements.

#55

ALAN PAGE

There was a certain fear associated with playing against the Minnesota Vikings during the late 1960s and early 1970s.

The Vikings had a marauding, tough, and nasty team that played in the winter elements at the dear, departed Metropolitan Stadium in Bloomington, located directly between the Twin Cities of Minneapolis and St. Paul.

While the Vikings had a hard-nosed offense led by Fran Tarkenton and running back Bill Brown, it was the defense that gave the team its identity. The Vikings attacked with power and speed, and while that defense played well as a whole, it was the defensive line that caused nightmares around the NFL.

Alan Page

That defensive line was known as the Purple People Eaters, and the best player in that stellar group was defensive tackle Alan Page.

Page and his partners Carl Eller, Jim Marshall, and Gary Larsen never were fans of their colorful nickname because it was not their style to promote themselves. That foursome was a business-minded group that simply wanted to win games and meet at the quarterback.

The Vikings of the late 1960s became the team to beat in the NFL once Vince Lombardi retired from the Green Bay Packers.. Lombardi was never afraid of an opponent, but perhaps he knew exactly what head coach Bud Grant was building in Minnesota with the Vikings.

The defense was capable of taking over any game and dominating for long stretches. They simply did not let opponents catch their breath once they started to attack. One of the primary keys to the defense was the ability of Page to be able to knife through the interior blocking of the offensive line and menace the quarterback.

Page was a consensus All-America player when he was drafted with the 15th pick in the first round by the Vikings. He won his starting job by the fourth game of the season, and he was firmly entrenched in the starting lineup before the end of his rookie season.

Page was basically unstoppable from his rookie year of 1967 though the 1976 season. He started to slow down a bit in 1977 and was released, but the Bears picked him up in 1978. He would remain in Chicago through 1981, when he would retire from the game. He was an incredibly durable player who never missed a game due to injury. He played in all 218 games he was eligible to put on a uniform.

Page was small by today's standards, as he played at 6-4 and 245 pounds. However, he had decent size for his era, and he was shockingly fast. If Page was able to get opposing offensive linemen off balance with a jab step, a hand punch, or any kind of move, he had won the battle. He would be by his man in an instant and on top of the quarterback.

Page was so good that he earned the NFL's MVP award and defensive player of the year in 1971. He is the only Vikings defensive player to win the league-wide MVP award.

He was a first-team All-Pro player six times and a nine-time Pro Bowler based on his consistent excellence.

Sacks were not an official stat throughout Page's career, but film review shows that he had 108.5 sacks while playing for the Vikings, and he went on to add 40 more during his run with the Bears. He had a career-best 18 sacks during the 1976 season, and he had six seasons win which he recorded double-digit sacks.

The remarkably quick Page recovered 22 fumbles in his career and he returned two of them for touchdowns. He also scored another touchdown on an interception return. Page was also a demon on special teams, as he blocked 28 kicks.

As much of a force as Page was as a pass rusher, he was just as good against the run. He understood blocking angles and leverage better than nearly every other defensive tackle, and he excelled at bringing down the ball carrier even when he was not in perfect position to deliver the big hit.

Page and his linemates, along with the Viking linebackers, made life miserable for opposing offenses. In addition to their game-altering speed, they often set up quarterbacks with stunts that often resulted in turnovers and sacks.

"When you play together like we have, you gain a lot of confidence in each other," Marshall told *Sports Illustrated* in 1969. "I know what Page is going to do and we react instinctively."

That's why the Vikings were so effective when they pulled their stunts. Page might give Eller or Marshall a look or a gesture just to let them know what he was seeing. That's when they would pull off stunts or fakes that would allow the Vikings to make game-changing plays.

Page has gone on to a stellar career in law in Minnesota since his playing days came to an end. He is an associate justice on the

Minnesota Supreme Court, and he has been an advocate for equal education for all youngsters through his Page Education Foundation.

While he is doing great things on the bench, his consistency in the NFL landed him a spot in the Pro Football Hall of Fame in Canton. He is one of the most deserving players in that shrine.

#56

JONATHAN OGDEN

The champion Baltimore Ravens of 2000 boasted one of the most dominant defensive units in the history of the NFL. They were Ray Lewis's team and the offense just went along for the ride. While Trent Dilfer manned the quarterback position—somebody had to do it—the offense was simply asked to not screw things up.

That assignment did not fall on left tackle Jonathan Ogden. The 6-foot-9, 340-pound stud drafted with the fourth overall pick in 1996 was a technician and a perfectionist. He dominated as a nasty run blocker and he quickly got the hang of pass blocking in the NFL. He was an 11-time Pro Bowl performer and a four-time All-Pro selection.

Jonathan Ogden

When Ogden's career came to an end following the 2007 season, many called him the greatest offensive player in the history of the Ravens franchise. Some compared him to Ray Lewis when it came to overall importance to the Ravens.

He was an important player to the team and he was also instrumental in getting the mainstream media and fans to pay more attention to what went on along the line of scrimmage. The Ravens clearly suffered as an offensive team throughout Ogden's era, but the more the team looked to upgrade the passing game and failed to reach that goal, the more Ogden performed at a level near perfection. The cameras of NFL Films regularly focused on what Ogden did in the trenches. His standard of performance put pressure on offensive linemen throughout the league.

Ogden's consistent performance made him one of the all-time greats, but he was never in it for personal glory. "He's a lineman. He's real humble; he's not in it for the fame," said Orlando Brown, who played alongside Ogden on the Ravens offensive line. "We want to be in it for the fame, but the camera doesn't look for us. The camera always did look at him because he was always doing his job at such a high level."

When Ogden was on the field, the left tackle became the star. He became such a force in every game that the Ravens fans started to look for him, regardless of who was running the ball or who was throwing it for them.

To think where the Ravens offense would have been without him is mind-boggling. Ogden was almost personally responsible for carrying the Ravens offense on his back. The 2003 season may have been his best year. That year, the 10–6 Ravens made the playoffs with the likes of Kyle Boller, Anthony Wright, and Chris Redman at quarterback. The Ravens had four games that season in which they gained less than 100 yards passing and only had three games in which they gained more than 200 yards passing.

Opponents threw for 550 yards more than the Ravens that season, yet Baltimore made the playoffs largely because Jamal Lewis ran for 2,066 yards. He did it primarily running behind Ogden. The offense was thoroughly predictable and went against the principle of teams needing to throw the ball to win, yet the Ravens found a way to be successful.

Ogden's presence on the other side of the line of scrimmage was always a wake-up call for his opponents. "Jonathan is one of the all-time best ever to play the position," said Miami Dolphins linebacker Joey Porter. "He always made me play at the highest of my abilities—otherwise he would embarrass me."

His consistency was not lost on the Ravens coaching staff, nor general manager Ozzie Newsome, who drafted Ogden in 1996. "I have been a lucky man to have played with and against some of the best players who have ever taken the field in the NFL," said Newsome, a Hall of Fame tight end. "I have also been able to watch some of the greatest players ever in my capacity as an executive for this team. I can say when it came to on-field performance, I have never seen any player do a better job than Jonathan Ogden. I don't care who the player is or what position he played, Jonathan's performance was always the best.

"Getting a chance to watch game films on Mondays after our games and watch him dominate week in and week out, it was something that always made you feel good. We had a lot of needs when we drafted Jonathan in 1996, but he was the best player in the draft and we got him. He paid us dividends for a long time."

During his peak, Ogden had formidable competition from Tony Boselli of the Jacksonville Jaguars and Orlando Pace of the St. Louis Rams. Boselli might have provided true competition for Ogden but knee injuries shortened his period of peak effectiveness. Pace was nearly as good as those two at his peak, but he seemed to fall off dramatically after the 2004 season. Pace would make his seventh

Jonathan Ogden

Pro Bowl in 2005, but that was not one of his better seasons and his reputation helped him make that team

Ogden decided to retire after 12 seasons because he felt like he could not perform to his own standards. "I never wanted to toot my own horn and tell everyone how great I was, but I will say that I did what I set out to do when the Ravens drafted me," Ogden said. "I feel like I did my job as professionally as possible and I feel good about the way I performed."

#57

MARCUS ALLEN

Al Davis proved he knew football a long time ago. After gaining control of the Oakland Raiders in the mid-1960s, Davis not only built a winning team but he did it with a philosophy that would serve the team well for more than three decades. Davis did it by bringing in a group of marauding, athletic players who would attack first and then attack again. Aggressiveness was the key word to describe the Raiders philosophy, both on the field and in the front office.

One of the best moves Davis ever made was drafting Heisman Trophy winner Marcus Allen of USC with the 10th pick of the first round of the 1982 draft. Allen had proved to be a worthy successor to O. J. Simpson at USC, a dominant running back who could take over a game with his speed, power, and sense for the moment. Like Simpson, when the Trojans needed a big play Allen always delivered.

Davis figured Allen would be a great back for his team as well. His speed, explosiveness, and ability as a receiver would help the Raiders continue their run as one of the elite teams in the NFL. Everything went according to plan. Allen ran for more than 1,000 yards in three of his first four seasons, including 1,759 yards and a 4.6 yards per carry average in 1985. He also caught 67 passes for 555 yards and won the league's MVP award that season. Two years earlier, he made the highlight-film play of Super Bowl XVIII when he reversed field, burst through the middle of the Washington Redskins line, and left everyone in his wake for a 74-yard touchdown that at the time was the longest run in Super Bowl history. He rushed for 191 yards—another record at the time—in the 38–9 rout of the Redskins.

Allen was one of the best running backs in the NFL, a Pro Bowl regular who was better than the sum of his considerable stats. By the end of his Hall of Fame career, he had amassed 12,243 rushing yards (10th all-time as of the writing of this book), 123 rushing touchdowns (third all-time), 145 total touchdowns (third all-time), and 17,654 yards from scrimmage (sixth all-time).

So how did it go bad for Allen and the Raiders?

For some unexplained reason, Davis fell out of love with Allen. First, he brought in former Navy running back Napoleon McCallum to share some of the running back responsibilities. And then came Bo. The Raiders had a chance to bring to bring in Heisman-winner Bo Jackson, one of the best athletes of the latter half of the 20th century. A star with the Kansas City Royals in baseball, Jackson was even more spectacular in his brief pro-football career because he was in many ways the best combination of speed and power since Simpson and perhaps Jim Brown.

It is understandable why Davis was enamored with Jackson. But he was injured in a 1990 playoff game against the Cincinnati Bengals and never made it back to the NFL, Davis continued to ignore Allen and forget that he was still a Hall of Fame worthy running back.

The situation came to a head when Allen called Davis out on national television during the 1992 season for burying him. "I think he's tried to ruin the latter part of my career," Allen told ABC's Al Michaels. "I think he's tried to devalue me."

The interview turned out to be one of the best moves of Allen's career. It showed the rest of the NFL that he still had the kind of fire he had shown in his first five years in the league. Even though he was 33 years old, Allen was determined to show that he was still a great back.

The Raiders' archrivals decided to give Allen an opportunity through free agency. The Kansas City Chiefs signed Allen as a free agent prior to the 1993 season and decided to build their offense around his running and receiving skills. He ran for 764 yards and 12 touchdowns and also caught 34 passes for 248 yards and three touchdowns in his first season in Kansas City. He gave the Chiefs the ability to finish drives with touchdowns, something that had been missing before Allen arrived. More importantly, the Chiefs won the AFC West title with an 11–5 record and the combination of Allen in the backfield and former San Francisco 49er Joe Montana behind center led the Chiefs to two postseason wins and a spot in the AFC title game against Buffalo, where the Chiefs dropped a 30–13 decision to the Bills.

While Davis lost faith in Allen—a development that he never explained publicly—Allen's teammates never stopped believing in him. Hall of Fame defensive end Howie Long, who was drafted by the Raiders the year before Allen, saw the running back as one of the most dependable players in the history of the game.

"In my mind, Allen was the most complete football player that I played with," Long said. "I would view Walter Payton as the most complete halfback of my generation, and I would put Marcus right up there in that category. Like Walter, Marcus excelled in every aspect of the game. You could always count on him.

"And then at the end of my career, I'm playing against him. I have to say it was one of the strangest experiences I ever had. When I saw Marcus in that Kansas City uniform, I had a hard time comprehending it. It didn't seem right to me."

But the Raiders' loss was the Chiefs' gain, and his ability to find the hole and make key plays impressed his teammates. "Marcus was just the consummate pro," Chiefs offensive guard Will Shields said. "He always made sure he took every play to the end zone during practice. He figured that was where the play was supposed to end, so that's where he finished every rep. It was his way of conditioning, but it was a mental-focus thing, too. It was his way of remembering how it felt to reach the end zone."

That ability impressed Kansas City head coach Marty Schottenheimer, who called Allen the best short-yardage runner in the history of the game. "I don't think he really liked me calling him that because he felt it sold him short a little bit," Schottenheimer explained. "But it was never meant to. He could do it all. But on those tough plays around the goal line or when you needed a yard and a half for a first down, Marcus is, was, and always will be the guy."

No disrespect intended.

#58

STEVE YOUNG

Steve Young has his name all over the NFL record book. He led the league in passing six times in his career, matching Sammy Baugh for the most times accomplishing that feat in NFL history. Young led the league four straight times, and no other quarterback has done it more than three consecutive times. His average of 8.0 yards per pass attempt ranks fifth all-time and he is the all-time career leader in passer rating, ahead of Peyton Manning, Kurt Warner, and, yes, Joe Montana.

The achievements and records are numerous but for everything he accomplished, Young was often treated as if he had shown up to the party uninvited.

Young was not an ogre nor did he have a Barry Bonds-like personality. He was cordial and helpful to the media and just as warm to his teammates, coaches and fans. But he did have one fault: He was not Montana.

Young came of age in the 1992 season. He completed 268 of 402 passes for 3,465 yards and 25 touchdowns against just seven interceptions. He also ran for 537 yards and four touchdowns. Despite his sensational numbers, Young could not win over the San Francisco 49ers fans, who were still enamored by the legend of Joe Montana. Young certainly understood the fans' passion and love for Montana. Any quarterback who leads his team to four Super Bowl titles has earned the loyalty that came his way. But sometimes that loyalty was marked by disdain for Young, and it was tough for the quarterback to endure.

"It's not like I ever thought I could just slide in here without anybody noticing," Young said. "Joe did so much with this team and it was natural for people to love him and want to see him under center. But when I started it became my job."

Young became a better quarterback in 1992 because of his confidence, maturity, and ability. But he also benefited from the coaching of Mike Shanahan, who was in his first season as offensive coordinator of the team.

Shanahan would of course go on to greater heights, winning two Super Bowls as head coach of the Denver Broncos. But when he got to San Francisco and had a chance to shape Young's career, he was the perfect man for the job. Shanahan knew that Young was a virtuoso talent and that the only thing he would have to do with him was make a few minor adjustments. One of those was to change his thought process when he decided to break the pocket.

Once Young had decided to run, he became a running back, using his speed and moves to elude or run by tacklers. Shanahan wanted him to remain a quarterback. "Just keep your eyes open as you approach the line of scrimmage," Shanahan told his quarterback. "Somebody may break loose and the big play may be there."

Young knew that, but hearing it from his coach slammed the message home. He no longer led with his legs or his arm. He led with his head and became one of the best quarterbacks in the game's history.

Going into the 1994 season, Young had played as well as any quarterback in the game but he had not won a Super Bowl. He knew that winning the title would decide his legacy, both in the minds of the fans as well as in his own.

"Whether you like it or not, one of the primary ways you are measured is through your titles," said Young. "Especially for a quarterback, and especially when you play for this team."

The 1994 Niners would prove to be one of the best offensive teams in NFL history, but it was in early-season losses to the Kansas City Chiefs and Philadelphia Eagles that the Niners came of age. In both games, Young was battered brutally by the opposing defenses but he never looked for the easy way out. The loss to the Chiefs—quarterbacked by an ancient Montana—had to be particularly galling but it was in the 40–8 home loss to the Eagles that Young showed his mettle.

It was clearly Philadelphia's day and they were treating Young with a sense of brutality as defensive end Reggie White had basically taken up residence in the 49ers backfield. He punished Young every time he got his hands on him. As the game got out of hand, head coach George Seifert was left with no choice but to replace him with Elvis Grbac.

The only problem was that Seifert didn't clear the substitution with his quarterback. Despite the physical abuse, Young had never even considered coming out of the game. He was not shy about letting Seifert know that he was displeased on the sidelines. He gave his coach an earful of his displeasure on the sidelines and that was the final bit of evidence needed to convince the Montana loyalists on the team that Young was a great leader. Not only did Young want to stay in the game, he also stood up for himself because he knew the move would be interpreted that the big loss was his fault.

"It was a very key moment," said Niners offensive lineman Jesse Sapolu. "Nobody could have blamed Steve if he had wanted to come out of the game. But to go off the way he did when the coach made the decision to take him out showed everybody how much he wanted it. He was a great quarterback who had the kind of desire and [work] ethic that matched his talent. That's awfully tough to beat."

The 1994 Niners would reel off 10 straight wins and wouldn't lose again until they dropped a meaningless Week 17 game in Minnesota. By that time, the Niners had won the NFC West and secured home field advantage throughout the NFC playoffs.

After a perfunctory 44–14 demolition of the Chicago Bears in the divisional playoffs, the Dallas Cowboys were unable to compete with the Niners. Deion Sanders gave the 49ers a much-needed boost against Cowboy receiver Michael Irvin and Young and Jerry Rice led the Niners to a 38-28 win that really was not as close as the final score would indicate.

That game was more of a test than the Super Bowl was. The San Diego Chargers had enjoyed a nice run to get to Miami and represent the AFC, but there was no way the Chargers had the firepower to hang in with the Niners.

The execution of the game plan was just as brutal as many of the observers had anticipated. Young threw touchdown passes to Rice and Ricky Watters early in the first quarter and the Niners rolled. Young was brilliant, completing 24 of 36 passes for 325 yard and set a Super Bowl record with six touchdown passes, three of them to Rice. But it wasn't just Young's passing that got the job done. He also gained 49 rushing yards and made plays with his feet whenever the overmatched Chargers thought they might be able to hem him in.

After the game, Young earned the Super Bowl MVP trophy for his spectacular performance. Elated with the win, Young had teammate Harris Barton help him remove an imaginary monkey from his back. The title that he needed to confirm his greatness had been well-earned and he was not going to let the moment pass without a ceremony.

Montana would always be a legendary Bay Area hero but that game gave Young the same status. He no longer had to prove anything to the doubters because his own championship team had been dramatic and impressive. Young had overcome Montana's great shadow and now had his own legion of fans to help him celebrate his great moment.

CAREER LEADERS IN PASSER RATING (THROUGH 2013 NFL SEASON)

Player	Rating
1. Aaron Rodgers	104.9
2. Peyton Manning	97.2
3. Steve Young	96.8
4. Philip Rivers	96.0
5. Tony Romo	95.8
6. Tom Brady	95.7
7. Drew Brees	95.3
8. Kurt Warner	93.7
9. Ben Roethlisberger	93.6
10. Joe Montana	92.3
11. Matt Ryan	90.6
12. Chad Pennington	90.1
13. Matt Schaub	89.8
14. Daunte Culpepper	87.8
15. Jeff Garcia	87.5

#59

CRIS CARTER

He was the second-best receiver to ever wear a Minnesota Vikings uniform and one of the best ever to play the game, but it didn't start out that way for Cris Carter. As a young receiver for the Philadelphia Eagles and Buddy Ryan, Carter considered himself an invincible player who could go out and party all week and do his job on Sunday. Dedication and conditioning—two factors he would be known for throughout his tenure in Minnesota—were not of interest to him in Philadelphia.

Carter's lack of dedication didn't show on the field, as he caught 11 touchdown passes in 1989. But Ryan was not impressed because he believed Carter was more interested in alcohol and drugs than he was in helping the Eagles win football games. In a move that shocked those outside Philadelphia, Ryan cut the productive Carter.

"Buddy Ryan told me he couldn't depend on me," Carter said. "He didn't know if I would flunk a drug test. He didn't know what I might do."

The move was the seminal moment in Carter's life and career. He did not like what he saw when he looked in the mirror.

"After I got cut, I was driving across the Walt Whitman Bridge," Carter said. "I had to call my wife and tell her I got cut. She was at home, pregnant with our first son. She had just graduated college and turned down a job offer to come to Philadelphia with me."

The devastated Carter realized his misfortune was all of his own doing. He vowed to clean himself up and hasn't had a drink since September 1990.

A receiver who can dominate in the red zone like Carter doesn't stay unemployed very long. The Vikings called the next day to sign Carter, and they picked up a bona fide all-time great.

Carter had excellent leaping ability and great athleticism, but lacked the great stopwatch speed that personnel people look for when scouting receivers. Once Carter got to Minnesota, he became a tireless worker who did everything he could to get better on an everyday basis. Combining his physical gifts with that relentless attitude helped turn Carter into one of the NFL's brightest stars.

During the 1994 season, Carter caught a league record 122 passes. He matched that total the following year, but Detroit's Herman Moore edged past his record with 123 receptions. Seven years after that, Colts virtuoso receiver Marvin Harrison caught 143 passes to become the single-season record holder.

Carter played in an era when San Francisco's Jerry Rice dominated and the Cowboys' Michael Irvin also made headlines. As a result, Carter was one of the league's most unappreciated superstars during the early part of his Minnesota career. However, all of his talents were cherished by head coach Dennis Green.

"I think Cris is more acrobatic and will make more difficult catches than those other guys," Green said. "You see a pass that you think he has no chance to catch because it's too high or will go out of bounds and then he does something that you don't believe. He'll dive for a ball and make a catch by scooping it or he will keep the tips of his toes in bounds while reaching over the barrier to make a catch. Nobody else can do it like Cris."

Carter excelled at all aspects of the game, but it was his hands that made him special. Carter regularly bathed his best assets in paraffin and oil to sooth them and relax them. He took care of them and pampered them during the week—and they took care of him on Sundays.

The diving catch? Nobody did it better than Carter. But that's just the start. Fingertip catches. Back-of-the-ball catches. One-handed diving catches. He was dominant in the red zone where he used his 6-foot-3, 220-pound frame and ability to catch anything he could get his hands on.

His trademark was the sideline catch, as he stretched like contortionist, his entire body out of bounds except for his tiptoeing feet. Nobody made those catches as often or as well as Carter.

A eight-time Pro Bowl selection, Carter's acrobatic catches helped etch his name into the NFL record books. As of the writing of this book, he stands third all-time in receptions (1,101), fourth in receiving touchdowns (130), and seventh in receiving yards (13,899).

The addition of Warren Moon to the Vikings lineup in 1994 may have provided the impetus Carter needed to go from star player to one of the league's all-time greats at the position. "Warren has meant a great deal to me," Carter said during the middle of the '94 season. "He's so professional and such an accurate passer. The trade we made to get him makes it a lot easier to do my job."

Carter, whose brother Butch played in the NBA for seven seasons, used a lot of basketball skills while on the football field. His athleticism, coordination, and ability to screen defensive backs from the ball were taken from his basketball instincts.

"You can tell a lot about a football player by the way he plays basketball," said former Vikings head coach Bud Grant, who played in the NBA during his younger years. "Some guys worry about catching the ball but Cris is beyond that. If Cris got a hand or a finger on it, you knew he was going to bring it in. He was concerned about what he would do before he caught the ball and after he caught it, but he didn't have to worry about catching it because he was so instinctive in that area."

As Carter established himself as one of the team's brightest stars, he took on more and more of a leadership role. Carter was not hesitant to tell the coaching staff if he thought the wrong play was called or to call out another player for making a mistake. Carter's emotional nature may have rubbed some of his teammates the wrong way, but it was an honest reaction that he refused to keep bottled up.

"I'm an emotional guy and when I get upset on the football field I have a reason," Carter said. "It was never about getting me the football more. If the tight end read the defense incorrectly, I'm all over the tight end. If the offensive coordinator calls a play that we didn't practice during the week, I'm questioning him on the sidelines."

Carter knew that his propensity for calling out players and coaches left him vulnerable if he didn't continue to perform at a high level. That provided Carter with even more motivation to stay on top of his game.

"I can stay in the position I'm in only if I play at a high level," he said. "If I don't, then I lose my voice in the locker room."

Carter's demanding attitude was forged by Ryan's decision to part company with him in Philadelphia. By showing his teammates "tough love" on a consistent basis, he was trying to force them to do their best on a consistent basis.

#60

TED HENDRICKS

It ended with one of the greatest upsets in Super Bowl history. The Los Angeles Raiders had been a solid team in 1983, winning the AFC West with a 12–4 record. They beat the Pittsburgh Steelers and Seattle Seahawks to earn a spot against the Washington Redskins in Super Bowl XVIII.

Not only were the Redskins the defending Super Bowl champions, they had rolled to a 14–2 record and had overwhelmed the Los Angeles Rams in divisional playoff round before holding off the San Francisco 49ers for the NFC championship.

While nearly everyone thought the Redskins would roll to a second straight title—the parade route had been planned and publicized—the Raiders whipped them from start to finish and came away with a 38–9 victory. At the end of the game, the cameras focused on Super Bowl MVP Marcus Allen and one of his teammates—Ted Hendricks.

Hendricks had been playing in the NFL since 1969, dominating the linebacker position with his size, quickness, and instincts. He had decided to call it a career at the end of the 1983 season and the upset win over the Redskins was the last game of his career.

Hendricks spent the bulk of his career with the Oakland Raiders. He had enjoyed an outstanding opening act in Baltimore and was traded to the Green Bay Packers for the 1974 season. He then moved to Oakland as a free agent in 1975 and he stayed with the Raiders until the end of his career.

Hendricks made a unique impression for every franchise he played for. He was a key part of the Baltimore Colts' Super Bowl V championship team in 1970 and then had one of his best seasons ever in 1971 when he had 5 interceptions and first showed the knack for blocking kicks that would be one of his signature moves throughout his career. He blocked a punt in a game against the Cleveland Browns and then later blocked an extra point against the New York Jets that was the difference in a 14–13 Baltimore win.

Hendricks had the unique gifts to be a great kick blocker. He was 6-foot-7 and had very long arms. Since he was so skinny—he played the bulk of his career at less than 220 pounds—he did not look like a typical football player. As a result, the nickname of "The Mad Stork" that had been given to him when he was a three-time All-American at the University of Miami stuck with him in the NFL.

Scouts had been impressed with Hendricks during his college career. There were concerns that he was too thin to play in the NFL but they had seen him tackle O. J. Simpson in a game against USC and they were impressed that Simpson had not gotten away from him. The Colts moved him from defensive end to linebacker to take advantage of his tackling ability.

Hendricks knew he was going to be successful in the NFL even if he did not carry the ideal weight. "Maybe I wasn't the prototype," Hendricks explained, "but once I got the experience of playing, I knew I could play in the big league. I have more leverage and though I may be giving up some speed, I can make up for it with my range. One of the problems in the NFL was that coaches were too programmed. They didn't think I could play linebacker at 214 [pounds] because no one else was playing the position at 214. Well, that is really quite silly. If you're good, you're good."

The Colts traded Hendricks to the Packers, and in his one season in Green Bay, Hendricks had five interceptions, blocked seven kicks, and scored a safety. Nevertheless, the Packers allowed Hendricks to leave after one season because he signed a free-agent contract with the Raiders. The Packers received two first-round draft choices from the Raiders as compensation, but it turned out to be a small price for one of the best linebackers in the history of the game.

Oakland head coach John Madden wasn't immediately taken with Hendricks, and he didn't get much of a chance to play regularly with the Raiders in 1975. "Well, we got him in some game situation and some special situations," Madden explained. "But let's face it, we made a mistake. He needed to be in there and that was that."

Madden and the other Raiders coaches had been fooled because Hendricks had been primarily a freelance player. He would read the play from his outside-linebacker position and react. Seemingly out of position, he almost never missed an opportunity to make a play.

In his 15-year career Hendricks blocked 25 field goals or extra points, an unofficial league record by a wide margin. He recovered 16 opponent fumbles and intercepted 26 passes, which he returned for 332 yards. He scored a record-tying four safeties, and recorded touchdowns on an interception, fumble return, and blocked punt.

"I like to think of myself as a complete football player," Hendricks said. "I was not a specialist. I could rush the passer and I could cover receivers. I made plays against the run and I liked playing on special teams. I don't how many linebackers today would do that. But that's how we played then and I think I did my job."

He was a four-time All-Pro and an eight-time Pro Bowler. He was voted into the Hall of Fame in 1990, proof that Hendricks had done his job quite well.

#61

KURT WARNER

Nobody looked at the quarterback from Northern Iowa and gave him any serious consideration.

Nobody associated with the NFL who scouted Kurt Warner at Northern Iowa in the 1992 and '93 seasons thought he had any kind of chance to be a decent pro quarterback.

Warner had been solid at Northern Iowa and proved himself to be an accurate passer when he completed 173 of 296 passes in his senior season. But Warner was not very athletic by NFL standards. He did not have a powerful arm. Scouts didn't realize how accurate he was, because his receivers often broke so wide open that all Warner had to do was get the ball in the same area code if he wanted to complete passes.

Warner refused to take no for an answer. He may not have had a chance to prove himself to NFL scouts and coaches, but he did get the opportunity to play in the Arena Football League. While the competition may not have been stellar, AFL quarterbacks have to get rid of the ball quickly, put it in a very small window, and show decisive leadership with every snap of the ball.

Warner played three years with the Iowa Barnstormers, and in his last two seasons with that team, he had touchdown-interception ratios of 61-15 and 79-14. Nobody could deny that Warner was accurate with his passes and that he made the correct decisions with the ball. He opened eyes around the NFL, and after playing one season with the Amsterdam Admirals in Europe, the St. Louis Rams gave Warner a chance to carry a clipboard and put on an NFL uniform.

Warner joined the Rams in 1998 and it appeared he would be a backup quarterback and little else. However, that script got torn up in the summer of 1999. Head coach Dick Vermeil liked the look of his team in training camp, and he thought the Rams would have a real chance to win the Super Bowl.

However, when starting quarterback Trent Green was lost for the year when he suffered a knee injury in a preseason game, it seemed that Vermeil's dreams went up in smoke. The Rams would now have to operate with Warner behind center.

Despite his success at the minor levels of the game, few thought Warner was ready for the big time. He was not a brilliant athlete, and he didn't have the pedigree to compete successfully against the best players in the game.

Vermeil, as was his style, tearfully told the media that his team would rally behind Warner and wouldn't miss a beat. However, it was hard to determine if Vermeil was trying to convince the media or himself.

But a funny thing happened when Warner took the field. He had Marshall Faulk on his side and a stellar receiving crew led by Isaac

Bruce and Torry Holt. Warner quickly realized he had superior talent on his side, and he wanted to take advantage of his opportunity.

He exceeded all expectations, and he did it by miles. He had a brilliant year, completing 325 of 499 passes for 4,353 yards with 41 touchdowns and 13 interceptions. The Rams were as powerful as Vermeil thought they would be, as they dominated the NFC.

The Rams not only won the NFC West, but also their 13-3 record was the best in the conference. They rocked the Minnesota Vikings in the divisional playoffs 49-37, and then played small ball as they edged the Tampa Bay Buccaneers by the unlikely score of 11-6 in the NFC Championship game.

Warner became the team's unquestioned leader. The former Arena Leaguer, who had spent his offseasons working in a grocery store, became one of the best quarterbacks in the NFL. It was an amazing rags-to-riches story, and the media was all over it.

However, to make the story complete, he had to come through in the Super Bowl against a strong Tennessee Titans team. The Super Bowl, of course, is often seen as the ultimate test for a quarterback. Skeptics thought Warner's lack of pedigree could come back to haunt him in the biggest game.

The Rams jumped out to a 16-0 lead in the Super Bowl, but the Titans charged back and tied the score in the late stages of the fourth quarter. The Rams got the ball back with two minutes to go, and this was Warner's chance to lead the Rams to the go-ahead score in the game.

Ideally, Warner would have led his team on a long drive and they would have kicked the winning field goal on the last play of regulation. However, Warner was not about leading his team to field goals. Instead, he hit Bruce with a 73-yard bomb and the Rams scored the go-ahead touchdown with 1:54 remaining.

While that gave the Titans time to mount a tying drive, the Rams' defense stopped them one yard short, and they held on for the victory. It is the only Super Bowl victory in the history of the franchise.

Warner went on to have two more remarkable years with the Rams before injuries started to limit him. He would move on to the New York Giants in 2004, and suffered through a disastrous season. The following year, Warner was picked up by the Arizona Cardinals.

He suffered through two mediocre and injury-torn seasons, but he started to throw the ball well again in 2007. By the 2008 season, Warner was finally healthy again and throwing the ball with superb accuracy. He completed 401 of 598 passes for 4,583 yards with 30 touchdowns and 14 interceptions. More importantly, the Cardinals became a winning team with a 9-7 record.

That was good enough to get them to the playoffs, and the Cardinals reeled off postseason victories over the Atlanta Falcons and Carolina Panthers before they defeated the Philadelphia Eagles in the NFC Championship game.

Warner was back in the Super Bowl, and this time he got to face the vicious Pittsburgh Steelers' defense. The Cardinals took the lead late in the fourth quarter when Warner hit star wide receiver Larry Fitzgerald with a 64-yard touchdown pass, but the Steelers staged their own game-winning rally and took the Vince Lombardi Trophy away.

Warner unexpectedly led two teams to the Super Bowl and won one championship and nearly a second. He proved himself to be perhaps the best undrafted player in the history of the game. He spent a career overcoming adversity and indignities to become one of the most accurate passers the game has ever seen.

#62

LaDAINIAN TOMLINSON

LaDainian Tomlinson was the dominant running back in the NFL throughout his first eight seasons, beginning in 2001.

Here's how good he was: In 2008, he rushed for 1,110 yards and 11 touchdowns on 292 carries. He also caught 52 passes for 426 yards and another touchdown.

It was clearly the worst season of his career up to that point.

Never mind that Tomlinson went severely downhill in 2009, and his career would come to an end after the 2011 season.

Through his first seven seasons in the league, Tomlinson had been part Walter Payton and part Barry Sanders. He was a running back who could catch passes like a wide receiver, who could block linebackers as if they were small children, and who could throw passes when he had to. He became the fourth fastest player to reach 10,000 rushing yards, accomplishing the feat in only his 106th NFL game, scoring 129 total touchdowns over those first seven seasons while throwing for seven more.

Tomlinson came into the league with a chip on his shoulder, because there were some who dismissed his monumental college career at Texas Christian because it was … well … at Texas Christian, where the level of competition wasn't perceived to be all that high. But few scouts who went to any of his games or studied his tapes echoed that opinion. They saw Tomlinson as a superhuman-type running back, a runner with springs in his legs that allowed him to jump out of tackles and get back to top speed in an instant.

"That's what I saw when I studied his college career," said the late John Butler on Chicago radio station WSCR in 2002. "He had this amazing ability to jump out of tackles and not just arm tackles. You just could not bring him down unless you got everything into the tackle and you were in almost perfect form. I didn't care if the WAC wasn't as good as the SEC or the Big 12. They certainly knew how to tackle and Tomlinson never went down easy."

Butler died in 2003, but it was not before he saw Tomlinson start to run roughshod over the NFL. Tomlinson's biggest fan was former Chargers head coach Marty Schottenheimer, who has always been enamored with the running game. He was never happier with a ground game than when he decided to give Tomlinson the ball. "In my opinion," Schottenheimer told the media, "LaDainian Tomlinson is the finest player ever to wear an NFL uniform."

Schottenheimer loved to speak in hyperbole, but he had a lot of evidence on his side when it came to Tomlinson.

Tomlinson's accomplishmentswere amazing and the comparisons with the game's all-time greats were valid. After a 1,236-yard rookie season in which he averaged only 3.6 yards per carry, Tomlinson warmed to the task of running in the NFL. He ran for 1,683 yards and

14 touchdowns his second year and 1,645 yards and 13 touchdowns in 2003. Those two mirror image seasons saw Tomlinson catch 179 passes and basically carry the Chargers. They were not yet a very good team, but they were getting closer and closer.

They would find their winning formula in 2004 with a 12-4 record that gave them first place in the AFC West. That season the Chargers were a little less dependent on Tomlinson, as he ran for 1,335 yards and an amazing 17 touchdowns. However, the Chargers got the balance they needed with a great season from Drew Brees at quarterback. It taught Tomlinson a lesson that having a winning record was more about spreading the wealth than about one player dominating the stat sheet.

"I will do whatever I can to win under all circumstances and every time I take the field," Tomlinson said. "But this is the NFL. The lessons have been learned time and time again. It's about balance and not being predictable. It's about running when your opponents think you are going to pass and passing when they think you are going to run. We learned that in 2004, as we were a lot more pre-dictable. We lost in the playoffs [in overtime to the Jets], but I think a lot of us got the message that the more you spread things around the better off you will be as a team."

It was clear that Tomlinson understood what it took to win in the NFL. However, Tomlinson did not always have the supporting cast in San Diego to allow him to take advantage of that knowledge. The 2006 season saw Tomlinson have one of the most magical years in NFL history, running for 1,815 yards, averaging 5.2 yards per carry, and pounding the ball into the endzone a league-record 28 times. He also caught 56 passes for 508 yards and 3 more touchdowns. That season was arguably the finest by any individual running back in NFL history.

The Chargers went 14-2 and were the No. 1 seed in the AFC playoffs, but they could not get by the New England Patriots, and that marked the end of the Schottenheimer era in San Diego. The coach had earned a reputation as a solid defensive leader and one who enjoyed the running game, but his inability to keep his cool on the sidelines in playoff games and his poor relationship with general manager A.J. Smith cost him his job.

That 2006 season also represented a changing of the guard as far as the national media was concerned. It was no longer whether Tomlinson was one of the greatest backs of all time. There was no doubt that he was. Even the great Walter Payton's supporters had to acknowledge that Tomlinson had brilliant numbers. But after 2006, how could Tomlinson ever match that form again? Questions would be raised. Was he on the downhill side of his career?

Those questions came at the same time that Tomlinson started to deal with nagging ankle and knee injuries. They weren't the kind that knocked him out of the lineup, but they were serious enough to slow him down. In 2007, Tomlinson injured his knee early in the divisional playoff win over Indianapolis and spent most of the game on the sidelines as the Chargers upset the Colts. In the AFC championship game, Tomlinson could not contribute against the Patriots.

He was not at his best in 2008, when he had his worst statistical season. But even at less than full strength, he posted numbers that 90 percent of the running backs in the NFL would have traded half their salary for.

Running backs are often considered to be done in the NFL after five or six years of hard running. Tomlinson had eight superior years, but that's when Father Time caught up with him.

He would eventually lose his job to Darren Sproles, and he finished his career with two substandard years with the New York Jets.

Tomlinson had a remarkable career, as he rushed for 13,684 yards (5th all-time) and 145 touchdowns (2nd all-time). If Tomlinson could have sustained his excellence two more seasons, he likely would have passed Payton and become the game's second-leading rusher and passed Emmitt Smith and become the league's all-time leader in rushing touchdowns.

But even without that type of status, the kid from TCU had a special career that will not soon be forgotten.

MOST CONSECUTIVE GAMES WITH A RUSHING TOUCHDOWN

Player	Year(s)	Team	Games
LaDainian Tomlinson	2004–2005	SD	18
John Riggins	1982–1983	WAS	13
George Rogers	1985–1986	WAS	13
Lenny Moore	1963–1964	BAL	11
Emmitt Smith	1994–1995	DAL	11
Emmitt Smith	1995	DAL	11
Priest Holmes	2002	KC	11

#63

BOBBY BELL

Bobby Bell could take over a game from the outside linebacker position and dominate on defense like few others.

In a game known for its brilliant athletes who can wow scouts with speed, leaping ability, and coordination, it's hard to find anybody who could top Bell. But aside from his athletic ability, Bell was a hardworking player who made the most of his God-given gifts and dominated on the field at the high school, college, and professional level.

Bell, of course, was one of the mainstays of Hank Stram's Kansas City Chiefs. He was one of the dominant figures on the football field every time he stepped on it, and while the American Football League was known for its high-scoring, light-up-the-scoreboard ways, there were some brilliant defensive players and Bell was perhaps their best.

Bell was so talented that he could play any position and be successful. Throughout his professional career, he played defensive line and linebacker, and Stram knew that Bell was going to dominate every time he went on the field.

Stram depended on Bell in every big-play situation his team found itself in to come through with a big play. Bell was never better than he was against the New York Jets in a 1969 playoff game.

With the Chiefs leading the game 6-3 in the fourth quarter, the Jets had the ball in a first-and-goal situation on the one-yard line.

It seemed obvious that the Jets were going to ram the ball into the endzone and take the lead. However, Bell and the Chiefs' defense rose up and stopped the Jets. Joe Namath gave the ball to the power-running fullback Matt Snell twice, but he could not overpower Bell and the Kansas City defense.

On the third-down play, Namath faked a handoff to Snell in an effort to draw Bell out of position. Bell wasn't buying and he stayed with Namath, and he prevented the Hall of Fame quarterback from throwing a touchdown pass. The Jets had to settle for a tying field goal.

That goal-line stand spurred on Len Dawson and the Chiefs offense. Kansas City drove the length of the field and scored the game-winning touchdown when Dawson hit wide receiver Gloster Richardson with a game-winning touchdown pass.

The Chiefs would then go on to beat the Oakland Raiders in the last AFL championship game before beating the Minnesota Vikings 23-7 in Super Bowl IV.

In that game, the heavily favored Vikings were expected to run all over the Chiefs and regain glory for the NFL. However, the Chiefs defense rebuffed and repulsed Minnesota, as the Vikings did not have the athleticism or speed to contend with active defensive players like Bell.

Whether he was playing in the American Football League or the NFL, Bell was dominant. He was a six-time AFL all-star, while he also made three NFL Pro Bowls after the two leagues merged prior to the 1970 season.

Bell was also named to the All-Time AFL first team. He recorded 40 sacks and 26 interceptions in his career, and he was elected to the Hall of Fame in 1983.

Bell was the first outside linebacker to be enshrined in the Hall, and when he was inducted into Canton, Stram called him the "greatest outside linebacker to ever play the game."

While Stram was given to hyperbole, there is every reason to believe that he may have been dead-on with his analysis. He was superb against the run, stellar in pass coverage, and he could rush the passer and cause havoc every time he went after the quarterback.

Additionally, he was a dominant player on special teams. Trying to return punts and kickoffs against the Chiefs was a near-hopeless task because Bell could run down the fastest return specialists, even when they had a big lead.

Bell returned six interceptions for touchdowns, and no linebacker has ever returned more picks for scores. Bell had the remarkable ability to read the quarterback's eyes, recognize where he was going to throw the ball, and then get to that spot at full speed just as the ball was arriving.

"I just marveled at his athletic ability," said Dawson. "I got to see him in practice every day, so I knew what he could do on the field, and I was just happy that I didn't have to play against him. There was no way anyone could get the better of him. He was as dominant at his position as any player I have ever seen."

#64

ADRIAN PETERSON

If Adrian Peterson played in a different era, he might be the most celebrated player in football.

Peterson is the best running back playing in the game. He is a sensational combination of speed, power, instinct, and desire. When Peterson is on his game, he is like a relentless machine who chews up yardage on a non-stop basis.

However, Peterson plays in a time where it's all about the passing game. Teams want a quarterback who can read defenses and throw the ball to multiple receivers so they can score quickly. They want big yardage after the catch and they want receivers who can leap over the defense to make plays.

The running game has become almost an afterthought for many teams. They want a running back who can convert first downs and touchdowns in short-yardage situations, and they also want to run the ball in the fourth quarter to keep the clock moving.

But the days of the bread-and-butter running attack appear to be over—for nearly every team but the Minnesota Vikings. The Vikings certainly want to have the same kind of passing options that top competitors like the Green Bay Packers and Chicago Bears have at their disposal, but they have a long way to go in order to get there.

But the Vikings have Peterson, and he is capable of taking over any game. He has done that since his rookie season in 2007 when he ran for 1,341 yards, averaged 5.6 yards per carry, and scored 12 rushing touchdowns. The Vikings had made Peterson the seventh pick in the first round, and they were not about to ease him into the lineup.

Peterson's ability to run over the strongest linebackers opened eyes all over the NFL, and it let Peterson know just what he was capable of doing against the best defensive players. "I couldn't wait to get to the NFL because I wanted the challenge," Peterson said. "I wanted to know how I would do when I had to play against the best. I had full confidence in my ability, but I still wanted to prove it."

He was at his best in a Week Eight game against the San Diego Chargers. Peterson set the NFL record with 296 rushing yards, which included 253 yards in the second half. Peterson had three rushing touchdowns, including a 46-yard scoring run midway through the fourth quarter that went a long way toward clinching a 35-17 Minnesota victory.

Brad Childress was coaching the Vikings that season, and he was known as a coach who wanted to use the passing game to give his team a chance. However, once he had Peterson on his side, he changed his philosophy.

"That's the way I like to play football," coach Brad Childress said. "I do have a healthy respect for being able to run it and taking somebody's will from them, and then playing off of that with play-action.

If you're looking for a benchmark, this is it." As good as Peterson's first year was, it proved to be an appetizer. His second year was just a superb example of the game's best running back finding his top gear. Peterson ran the ball 363 times for 1,760 yards and he scored 10 touchdowns.

Peterson was just a workhorse that second season, as he averaged nearly 23 carries per game. Peterson simply wanted the ball every time he could get it, and he tried to carry the 10-6 Vikings on his back. Minnesota made the playoffs in 2008, but they were knocked out in the Wild-Card round by the Philadelphia Eagles.

Peterson was nearly as good the following season when he ran for 1,383 yards and an amazing 18 touchdowns that made him the lord of the manor for all of his fantasy football owners. He followed that season with a 1,298-yard season in 2010, and he also scored 12 touchdowns that year.

Disaster struck Peterson in 2011, as he had rushed for 970 yards and 12 touchdowns when he went down with an ACL injury in a 33-26 victory over the Washington Redskins in Week 16. The fact that the injury happened so late in the season appeared to be a major problem because it didn't look like he would have a chance of being ready for the opening of the 2012 season.

Peterson told the Vikings and the media that he would be ready for the start of the season, and his conditioning and workout regimen at least gave him a puncher's chance of being ready for the year. As the preseason moved along, few thought he would be ready, but Peterson was in the lineup for the opening game against the Jacksonville Jaguars and he ran for a very competent 84 yards and two touchdowns.

Peterson was not at his best for that game, but he would find his top gear in Week Seven when he ran for 153 yards against the Arizona Cardinals. That was the first of eight consecutive 100-plus-yard games for Peterson. He would run for 210 yards against the Packers in early December and 212 yards versus the Rams two weeks later. He would add 199 yards in the regular-season finale against Green Bay, and that would give him 2,097 yards for the year.

The Vikings would also earn a playoff spot that season even though they had one of the most inept passing attacks in the league. It didn't matter, as Peterson simply carried his team on his shoulders even though he was coming off a brutal injury.

Peterson's performance earned him the NFL's MVP Award, the Bert Bell Award, and the Associated Press Offensive Player of the Year Award.

It was a season that few thought was possible even under the best of circumstances, let alone coming so soon after a major injury.

It was the kind of season that allowed Peterson to join company with the game's best all-time running backs. He deserved to be mentioned with the likes of Earl Campbell, Gale Sayers, and Emmitt Smith, and perhaps just beneath Jim Brown, Barry Sanders, and Walter Payton.

Going into the 2014 season, Peterson has seven years under his belt. The history book says that running backs often start to lose their effectiveness after six, seven, or eight years.

If that's the case, Peterson may no longer be the warhorse he has been. However, he's so strong, fast, powerful, and skilled, that he just may break that trend and join the very best running backs that have ever played the game.

#65

CURTIS MARTIN

Curtis Martin was a blue-collar superstar throughout the whole of his brilliant 11-year career in the NFL.

Martin was never considered one of the glamour players in the league and many would never put his name in the same category with Jim Brown, Walter Payton, Barry Sanders, Emmitt Smith, and Eric Dickerson.

However, Martin earned his spot with the pantheon of the game's greatest running backs because of his productivity. Smith, Payton, and Sanders are on top of the all-time rushing yardage list, but Martin ranks fourth on the list of all-time productive runners with 14,101 yards.

Martin started his career with the Patriots when they drafted him in 1995. He was a dynamic back for them in each of his first three years, rushing for 1,487 yards in his rookie year and following that up with seasons of 1,152 and 1,160 yards. Martin had been a touchdown machine in his first two seasons, as he had 14 scores in each of those years.

Martin had signed a three-year contract with the Patriots after he had been drafted out of Pittsburgh following his brilliant college career, and he was a restricted free agent as the 1998 offseason began.

If any team wanted to sign a restricted free agent, the agent's original team would be due heavy-duty compensation in the form of draft picks. That type of high tariff nearly always prevented NFL teams from signing those type of free agents, no matter how talented the player.

But Bill Parcells, Martin's original coach with the New England Patriots, had moved on to the Jets by that point. When the chance to sign Martin came up, Parcells didn't hesitate. Remember, Parcells had longed to serve as his own personnel man, and the opportunity to bring a talent like Martin aboard was just the kind of opportunity he was hoping for when he decided to man the general manager position. Martin's play and determination would help define Parcells's stewardship of the Jets franchise.

The Jets gave Martin a five-year, $36.24 million contract, and they gave the Patriots first- and third-round draft picks.

Many in the NFL thought the Jets had given up far too much for a running back, but it turned out to be a bargain.

Parcells knew Martin was worth the price.

"I certainly recognize the price is a formidable price to pay for the player, but to me this was a question of a known vs. the unknown," Parcells told the *Hartford Courant* at the time of the signing. "And those draft choices, although I would term them important, they're only pawns right now." Martin would string together 10 consecutive seasons with 1,000 rushing yards or more to start his career. The only year in which he did not reach that figure was 2005, which turned out to be the final year of his career. He still rushed for 735 yards in his swan song.

Martin did not have sprinter's speed or Olympic-type athletic ability, but he was the ideal running back because he was quick, smart, tough, and opportunistic. He knew the tendencies of his opponents, and that allowed him to make big plays any time he got into the open.

Martin's first instinct was to initiate contact with defenders. He ran with good speed and leverage, and that allowed him to pound opponents and push them backwards.

A lot of good running backs will start off a game in that manner, but as the game reaches the second quarter or later, they begin to tire or lose their effectiveness. Martin simply would never stop pounding, and that was one of the major keys to his consistency.

Martin was as well-liked off the field as he was effective on the field. He left the NFL with a boatload of friends and supporters, as he had earned nothing but respect for the way he played and carried himself.

There were no enemies. Owner Robert Kraft of the Patriots always respected Martin, even after he left his team following the 1997 season.

"The key to life is having quality people with you, and Curtis is right at the top of the heap as a quality individual, both the way he conducts himself personally and the way he played," Patriots owner Robert Kraft told ESPN New York when Martin went into the Hall of Fame in 2012. "I will forever have a warm spot in my heart for him. The Jets made a very wise decision by getting him. I just wish he were entering the Hall of Fame as 100 percent Patriot." It is the rare individual who can travel a path that leads to universal respect, from friends and competitors alike. Yet, that's just what Martin did and it earned him a spot among the 65 greatest players of all-time.

POSITIONAL RANKINGS

QUARTERBACK
1. Joe Montana
2. Johnny Unitas
3. Peyton Manning
4. Tom Brady
5. Brett Favre
6. John Elway
7. Dan Marino
8. Otto Graham
9. Roger Staubach
10. Bart Starr
11. Fran Tarkenton
12. Steve Young
13. Kurt Warner

RUNNING BACK
1. Jim Brown
2. Walter Payton
3. Barry Sanders
4. Earl Campbell
5. Gale Sayers
6. Emmitt Smith
7. Eric Dickerson
8. Thurman Thomas
9. O.J. Simpson
10. Marshall Faulk
11. Tony Dorsett
12. Marcus Allen
13. LaDainian Tomlinson
14. Curtis Martin

WIDE RECEIVER
1. Jerry Rice
2. Randy Moss
3. Lance Alworth
4. Cris Carter

TIGHT END
1. Kellen Winslow
2. John Mackey
3. Mike Ditka
4. Tony Gonzalez

OFFENSIVE LINE
1. Anthony Munoz (OT)
2. John Hannah (OG)
3. Jim Parker (OG/OT)
4. Forrest Gregg (OT/OG)
5. Gene Upshaw (OG)
6. Jonathan Ogden (OT)

DEFENSIVE LINE
1. Deacon Jones (DE)
2. Reggie White (DE)
3. Bob Lilly (DT)
4. Joe Greene (DT)
5. Bruce Smith (DE)
6. Merlin Olsen (DE)
7. Willie Davis (DE)
8. Alan Page (DT)

LINEBACKER
1. Lawrence Taylor (OLB)
2. Dick Butkus (MLB)
3. Ray Lewis (MLB)
4. Junior Seau (MLB)
5. Chuck Bednarik (MLB/C)
6. Jack Lambert (MLB)
7. Ted Hendricks (OLB)
8. Ray Nitschke (MLB)
9. Bobby Bell (OLB)

DEFENSIVE BACK
1. Ronnie Lott (S/CB)
2. Mel Blount (CB)
3. Deion Sanders (CB/KR)
4. Darrell Green (CB)
5. Ken Houston (S)
6. Rod Woodson (CB/S)
7. Ed Reed (S)

JUST MISSED

There's room to argue. We understand that. I had plenty of arguments with myself while compiling this top 65 list. Players that failed to make the top 65 are still great players. We understand that.

How do you leave off a quarterback like Drew Brees, who ranks fifth all-time in passing yardage heading into the 2014 season and is one of the most accurate passers in the game? What about Aaron Rodgers, who is simply unstoppable when he gets on a roll? Bert Jones had perhaps the strongest arm of any quarterback not named Dan Marino, while Sonny Jurgensen and Lenny Dawson were great leaders who may not have been great athletes but found a way to come through when it mattered most.

As we look at the other positions, it's hard not to mention a back like Jerome Bettis who clearly left everything he had on the field, and is the 6th-leading rusher in NFL history. Jim Taylor was the best running back on Vince Lombardi's Green Bay Packers. He did the heavy work inside and could also take it on the power sweep through the alley provided by Green Bay's great blocking. Marion Motley was the equivalent of a tank in a football uniform. Injuries kept Seattle Seahawks running back Curt Warner from achieving greatness.

Some believe that Green Bay's Don Hutson was the best receiver the game has ever seen until Jerry Rice came along. Tim Brown may not have been much of a technician as a route runner—his own admission—but he caught everything he touched. Was there ever a more thrilling sight than Raider tight end Dave Casper tracking an over-the-head pass from Ken Stabler?

Jackie Slater was a ferocious blocker who was smarter than 99 percent of the defensive ends who tried to beat him. Mick Tinglehoff was small compared to the men he had to block, but he was always quicker than his opponents, a fact that pleased Minnesota Vikings head coach Bud Grant.

Doug Atkins and Gino Marchetti were two of the strongest men to ever play on the defensive line and two of the most underrated. Buck Buchanan was hidden away in the American Football League, but he dominated with speed and strength.

Rickey Jackson was unlucky to play at the same time as Lawrence Taylor. Jackson was an awesome player, but L.T. overshadowed him throughout their careers. Dave Robinson may have been the most underappreciated player on Vince Lombardi's Packers. He simply never missed a tackle.

Paul Krause was the greatest interceptor in league history. Dick "Night Train" Lane was a spectacular interceptor and a ferocious tackler. Jimmy Johnson was a cover corner before the term had been invented. Kenny Easley would have been the equal of Ronnie Lott had injuries not devastated his career.

Though I agonized over many of my selections, I couldn't include everyone who seems deserving of making the list. Therefore, here's a secondary list of those players who just missed the cut.

JUST MISSED:

QB: Sonny Jurgensen, Len Dawson, Bert Jones, Ken Anderson, Dan Fouts, Y.A. Tittle, Sid Luckman, Terry Bradshaw, Warren Moon.

RB: Jim Taylor, Franco Harris, Lenny Moore, Joe Perry Ricky Watters, Marion Motley, Roger Craig, Curt Warner.

Receiver: Don Hutson, Raymond Berry, Steve Largent, James Lofton, Tim Brown, Art Monk, Marvin Harrison, Fred Biletnikoff, Lynn Swann, Michael Irvin, TE Ozzie Newsome, Terrell Owens, TE Shannon Sharpe, John Stallworth, TE Dave Casper.

Offensive line: Bob "Boomer" Brown, Jackie Slater, Dwight Stephenson, Mick Tingelhoff, Willie Roaf, Larry Allen, Dan Dierdorf, Mike Webster, Roosevelt Brown, At Shell, Bruce Matthews, Jim Otto, Orlando Pace.

Defensive linemen: Jack Youngblood, Carl Eller, Doug Atkins, Buck Buchanan, Gino Marchetti, Andy Robustelli, Kevin Greene, Michael Strahan

Linebacker: Ray Nitschke, Harry Carson, Derrick Thomas, Sam Huff, Derrick Brooks, Pat Swilling, Rickey Jackson, Chuck Howley, Dave Robinson.

Defensive back: Dick "Night Train" Lane, Paul Krause, Emlen Tunnell, Johnny Robinson, Larry Wilson, Jimmy Johnson, Kenny Easley, Ed Reed.

Kicker: Lou "The Toe" Groza (OL), Jan Stenerud, Morten Andersen, P Ray Guy, Sammy Baugh (QB)

ACKNOWLEDGMENTS

I have been very lucky. I knew what I was going to do with my life by the time I was in eighth grade. Before that, I had dreams of becoming a major league athlete, but reality hit hard by the time I was 14. I was average at best, and the idea of getting paid to play had been put to bed before I got into high school.

My mother Gloria was a writer herself and she encouraged me at every turn. One of the things she did was send me letters every day when I went to overnight camp. She included the game story, the box score, and the standings that came in the Newark (N.J.) *Star-Ledger* every day. I was a Yankee fan (then—not now) and her diligence allowed me to keep up with my favorite team. As I read Jim Ogle's account of some very ordinary Yankee teams, I realized he was being paid to watch and chronicle those Yankee teams. That's how he made his living. And that's how I would do it.

I got my first real opportunity with a paper called the *New Brunswick* (N.J.) *Home News.* Most of the time, I was covering high school events—football, basketball, and baseball—but before the start of the 1981 NFL season, the sports editor held a department meeting. He spelled out the expectations of the paper for a group of young sportswriters. Just as the meeting was about to break up, he added one more thing. "We have to cover the Giants this year," he said glumly. "Does anybody want to cover the game this Sunday?"

My hand shot up almost uncontrollably. Shockingly, nobody else was interested. I got the press pass and that was the beginning of my career covering pro football. The Giants returned to glory that year, making the playoffs for the first time since 1963. I was there when they won the last game of the season in overtime against the Dallas Cowboys to clinch a playoff spot. It was a long time ago. Lawrence Taylor was a rookie and Bill Parcells was an assistant coach who would smile at and talk to reporters, on occasion.

After putting my career on hold while I pursued my Masters degree in journalism at Northwestern, I got an opportunity to cover the NFL at *Pro Football Weekly* for 10 years. Publisher Hub Arkush was an excellent boss who ran a great paper. I worked with outstanding writers throughout the country and there was a great in-house staff that included Bob LeGere, Bob Peters, Rick Korch, Neil Warner, Ron Pollack, and the late Joel Buchsbaum.

During my time at *Pro Football Weekly* I was completely immersed in the game. I was able to talk to many of the great stars and coaches in the game and many of the key decision makers as well. I received personal letters from Wellington Mara and Lamar Hunt, and spoke with coaches such as Chuck Noll, Don Shula, Jimmy Johnson, Chuck Knox, and Bill Belichick. Here's a funny story about Belichick. He's not supposed to be of much use to the media, but he once called me at home after midnight to give me an interview.

It was a long time ago and I was married at the time, and I explained to Bill that I was happy that he called, but it was a tad late. When he gave me the option of ending the interview right then and there or continuing, I decided not to let the opportunity pass. I talked to him for 20 minutes.

I have had the opportunity to speak to many of the great stars mentioned in this book throughout the years. After I left *Pro Football Weekly*,

I have continued to write about football for magazines, newspapers and websites and it has been my great joy. I thank the many great media relations people around the league and the players and coaches who have been very generous with their time.

You get into a business like this at a young age because there is something magical about these sports that you love. Most of us start out playing baseball or football at a young age, and only the best survive. To have the chance to cover these individuals has been a dream come true.

INDEX

Index

Index

Index

Index